Letters by Lamplight

Anna Louisa Wellington Stoner (1857–1953), 1914. Reproduced by permission of Mary Margaret Stoner McLean, Arlington, Texas.

Letters by Lamplight

*A Woman's View of Everyday Life
in South Texas, 1873–1883*

LOIS E. MYERS

Baylor University Press
Waco, Texas

First paperback edition: 1998 / ISBN 0-918954-69-X

Copyright © 1991 by
BAYLOR UNIVERSITY PRESS
Waco, Texas 76798
All Rights Reserved

Portions of Chapters 1 and 2 appear in Lois E. Myers, "He Couldn't Get along Without a Wife: A Woman's View of Married Life in Victoria County, 1877–1881," The Journal of South Texas 1 (Spring 1988): 11–33.

The Library of Congress has catalogued the hardcover edition of this work as follows:

Myers, Lois E., 1946–
    Letters by lamplight : a woman's view of everyday life in
    South Texas, 1873–1883 / Lois E. Myers.
        p.   cm.
    Includes bibliographical references and index.
    ISBN 0-918954-53-3 (alk. paper)
    1. Stoner, Anna Louisa Wellington—Correspondence.
    2. Women pioneers—Texas—Correspondence. 3. Texas—
    Social life and customs. 4. Frontier and pioneer life—
    Texas. I. Title.
    F391.M94 1991
    976.4'061—dc20   90-85476
                                                          CIP

Cover drawing by A. Kay Jacobs.

Printed in the United States of America on acid-free paper.

Contents

Preface

The study of the past is much more complex than once thought. Social historians have come to realize that history happens to everyone, regardless of age, race, class, or gender. They are now asking new questions and turning to new resources in order to understand the relationships between historical change and ordinary lives and everyday experience. In order to comprehend the lives of non-privileged persons, who because of legal, social, political, or economic disadvantage left behind little public record, historians investigate private testimony, revealed in both written and oral narratives.

Throughout Texas history, women told their life stories—to each other, to their daughters, to their granddaughters—through journals, diaries, letters, autobiographies, and oral tradition. Many personal narratives of Texas women became lost through the years because they were not valued or protected, but some have come to light from the depths of trunks stored away in attics, from shoe boxes in garages, and from shelves of library archives. As more and more evidence of the lives of individual Texas women surfaces, social historians can begin unraveling the connections between women and history. Because women's lives intertwine with home, family, and social group, learning their history also reveals the past experiences of children, families, domestic life, kinship relations, homemaking skills, courtship, widowhood, and social, charitable, educational, and religious groups.

This book recounts the everyday experiences of one Texas

woman, Anna Louisa Wellington Stoner, as related in her own words in letters written during the post-Reconstruction era. Anna's letters, along with those of her correspondents, paint a detailed portrait of one family's response to vast economic and social transformations taking place throughout Texas following the Civil War. Woven together, Anna's narratives tell the story of a young woman's development from school girl to farm wife to pioneer rancher. In addition to commonplace details of home, work, and family life, they provide insights into neighborhood and community relationships. Paraphrased and quoted passages from the letters form the nucleus of this book; surrounding that center, and occasionally interfusing it, is supportive information from public records, contemporary writings, and published histories that place Anna's narratives within their historical and geographical context.

Anna Stoner's correspondence is preserved in the Wellington-Stoner-McLean Papers in The Texas Collection of Baylor University, Waco, Texas. The larger compilation of materials includes letters, legal and business papers, journals, artifacts, and photographs of Anna's ancestors and descendants alike, encompassing a time frame from 1831 to the present. The earlier resources in the collection provide important materials for grasping Anna's family background, and some of the later papers aid in reconstructing her later life. However, a group of eighty-six letters written between Anna and her mother and brother from 1873 to 1883 is unique within the collection because it contains letters from both sides of the exchange. Anna's mother and brother kept the majority of the letters written to them by Anna; likewise, Anna preserved most of the letters written to her from her mother and brother. Their correspondence came to an abrupt end upon the death of Anna's brother, after which her mother became a member of the Stoner household. This particular body of letters provides an in-depth, well-documented view of one Texas family's response to historical change.

The extant letters of Anna and her family during the 1870s and 1880s cover a wide area of the South Texas landscape, from Refugio and Victoria counties on the Gulf Coast to Edwards and Uvalde counties in the west. Farming and ranching dominated South Texas when Anna Wellington Stoner lived there over a century ago. Today, where her father planted cotton and corn with slave labor in Refugio County, silhouettes of oil and gas machinery rise from the prairie. In Victoria County, near where she tended her garden and fed chickens on rented farmland, a petrochemical plant stands on the banks of the Guadalupe River. Nestled in the Nueces River canyon that forms the boundary of Edwards and Real counties, between the villages Anna knew as Dixie and Bull Head, a high adobe wall, several feet thick and topped with broken glass, surrounds the grounds and stables of an elaborate Arabian horse farm. Around the bend lies an exotic game ranch. In the lower Nueces River canyon in Uvalde County, the Stoner Ranch, founded by Anna in 1884, has changed the least perhaps, except for the stark white satellite dish in the yard of her grandson's home.

Uncovering Anna Stoner's past required the assistance of many people, to whom I am indebted. From my initial interest in the history of the American West, I was guided into social history and western women's history, in particular, by Professor Thomas L. Charlton, of the Department of History, Baylor University. Dr. Charlton encouraged me to ask new questions and seek new resources. Through the generous help of archivists, librarians, and county clerks in Texas and Arkansas, I located those new resources. In particular, I am grateful to Kent Keeth, Ellen K. Brown, and Kathleen Hinton, of The Texas Collection, for bringing Anna's letters to my attention, and then retrieving files, adjusting magnifying lamps, and cleaning Nueces River silt from delicate, century-old papers. Michael Toon and Richard Veit, also of The Texas Collection, assisted in locating supportive materials for establishing the historical and geographical setting of Anna's life. Likewise, Mary Madearis and the staff of the Southwest Arkansas Regional Archives, in Washington, aided my research into Anna's family background. Librarians, county clerks, and historical societies in Refugio, Victoria, Uvalde, Edwards and Real counties of Texas also contributed valuable information.

One of the greatest rewards of my research was getting to know three of Anna Stoner's grandchildren: Margaret Stoner McLean, Michael Lowery Stoner, and Royal Clinton Stoner. I am deeply indebted to Margaret, Mike, and Red for recognizing the historical importance of Anna's papers, for depositing them in the archives of Baylor University, and for encouraging me in my research. We spent many hours together over the past three years, recording their memories of their grandmother, their parents, and their lives on the Stoner Ranch. Their recollections of family oral tradition greatly enhance this study.

Furthermore, I am indebted to several scholars who critiqued this study and offered helpful advice and encouragement. They are Susan H. Armitage, Director of American Studies at Washington State University; Margaret Jones Bolsterli, of the Department of English at The University of Arkansas at Fayetteville; Malcolm D. McLean, Director of the Robertson Colony Collection at The University of Texas at Arlington; and Gerald D. Saxon, Assistant Director for Special Collections at The University of Texas at Arlington.

Only a few photographs related to Anna's life during the period of this study survived to the present. I am, therefore, very grateful to artist A. Kay Jacobs for her creative sketches, which enrich our image of the setting in which Anna lived and wrote. Likewise, Brad Parish's carefully detailed maps aid our understanding of nineteenth-century Arkansas and Texas, where small communities, many now abandoned, punctuated the landscape.

Preface

The empathy I share with Anna and other Texas women resides in my own life as daughter, wife, and mother. I gratefully acknowledge the inspiration given by my parents, Mary Ellen and L. A. Smith, Jr.; the steadfast encouragement of my husband, Dennis R. Myers; and the cheerful cooperation of my children, Lori and David.

Lois E. Myers
Waco, Texas

Letters by Lamplight

Introduction

F or nearly eighty years, from Reconstruction to post-World War II, Anna Louisa Wellington Stoner expressed through letters her personal impressions of life in South Texas, experienced first as a farm wife in a well-populated rural neighborhood, then as a pioneer in a sparsely-settled frontier setting, and finally as a widowed rancher on her own river canyon ranch. Originally collected by her mother, frantically saved from a Nueces River flood by her son, carefully cleaned and preserved by her granddaughter, Anna's extant papers embody a compelling human drama of one family's triumphs and tragedies through several generations. Anna's personal correspondence from the early 1870s to the late 1940s is now part of the Wellington-Stoner-McLean Papers in The Texas Collection of Baylor University, Waco, Texas. Within the rich historical treasures of Anna's family papers lies an especially significant compilation of eighty-six letters exchanged between Anna Stoner and her mother and brother during the 1870s and 1880s. These letters, the basis for this study, record for historians the shared values and commonplace activities of one South Texas family as it responded to rapid economic and social changes occurring in the post-Reconstruction era.

Anna Stoner's personal letters are narrow in scope, reflecting the circumscribed world of most American women of her day, but they expose a profoundly honest, feminine perspective on nineteenth-century rural and frontier family life in Texas. Women's accommodations to life events, such as births, deaths, and migrations, shaped the family, and the resilient adjustment of the family to economic, political, and social transitions created the community. Therefore, visualizing the conditions of the average woman's life and work from her own viewpoint illuminates the dynamics of both family adaptation and community evolution. However, because nineteenth-century law and custom restricted women politically and economically, public documentation of individual women's lives and work remains scarce. Demographic data provide a composite view of the external facts of women's lives in the past, but feminine testimony expands the collective view by revealing women's private thoughts, emotions, and self-images. In fact, women's personal literature is often the only recorded legacy that provides insights into the intimate details of home life in the previous century. Besides broadening our understanding of human experience, women's personal literature of the past enhances the self-concepts of women in the present, both individually and collectively. Until recently, women's collective historical memory formed around stereotypes espoused in gender-biased traditional histories which focused upon political and military events. The ordinary woman could seldom relate her complex and varied everyday experiences to the few mythical superwomen in the history texts. Viewing the everyday experiences of the past through the eyes of women of various ethnic and social groups corrects the false impressions of traditional historiography and verifies the bonds between women of the past and the present.

In the 1970s historians of the American West began reassessing women's private writings in an effort to explain the role of women in the story of westward expansion and settlement.[1] Initially, frontier women's personal documents exposed significant discrepancies between the experiences of real women and the single dimension stereotypes of women in traditional western histories, popular culture, and literature.[2] Some historians applied Frederick Jackson Turner's frontier thesis to women's private writings to determine the extent to which the frontier experience liberated women by challenging their traditional cultural roles.[3] Delving deeper into art, literature, and public records, in addition to personal writings, other historians discovered that while gender roles of frontier women varied somewhat according to their racial and cultural backgrounds, all western women shared in common the struggles of daily survival, of maintaining family continuity, and of establishing enduring social relationships.[4] Progressively, historical scrutiny of women's roles in the western United States has come to play an integral role within scholarly institutions, associations, and publications. In the course of two decades, feminist historians have dispelled myths and established women's distinctiveness in the West, ethnicists have opened new understandings of both cultural diversity and cultural continuity, and social historians have proven the significance of nontraditional sources of historical evidence, including women's personal writings.

Like diaries, journals, and autobiographies, women's letters furnish valuable, introspective reminiscences. Letters are literature; they conform to a formal structure, use conventional imagery, and have a narrative sense. They contain irony and solicit an emotional response that connects reader and author. Through letters, nineteenth-century women expressed their inner voices at a time when they were discouraged from writing professionally. For women facing the uncertainty of the frontier, correspondence with relatives separated by great distances provided a sense of order and continuity. Also, correspondence with friends fostered a sense of shared community among widely scattered acquaintances. To migrating families, letters were a tenuous link between the known and the unknown. Responsibility for keeping that connection viable, even as successive migrations worked to break it apart, fell chiefly upon women.[5]

From the time families from the United States and other foreign countries first colonized Texas, women wrote letters describing their new lives on the frontier. The descriptions of early Texas as an Eden-like paradise in the letters of Mary Austin Holley, published widely during the 1820s and 1830s, inspired generations of Anglo-Americans to settle in Texas. Later, the letters of Norwegian emigrant Elise Waerenskjold, published in newspapers throughout her native country, attracted northern European families to Texas. Likewise, German women migrating into the Texas Hill Country wrote letters and reminiscences to relatives and friends telling about everyday experiences in their new home. In letters to Ireland, Catholic nuns teaching in San Antonio in the 1850s left an important record of early education in Texas. After families settled in Texas, temporary separations of individual family members, traveling for reasons of pleasure, business, or war, provided further opportunities for correspondence. A few small collections of extant letters of nineteenth-century Texas women have appeared in publications, but the majority remains unpublished, awaiting discovery in archives or among personal papers held by descendants.[6]

The use of personal letters as primary documents for historic investigation raises serious methodological questions concerning accessibility and validity. Private letters of persons belonging to those populations traditionally devalued by their culture are rarely available, including those written by nineteenth-century women outside the privileged class. Rarer still are correspondence collections in which letters from both sides of the exchange exist. Also, letters represent, in a sense, already-interpreted history. Subjective memory plays an important role in determining what is written. Letters are testimony; they reflect the author's personal ideas about events. Obviously, letters illustrate the viewpoints of literate persons, who in the nineteenth century were predominantly white, educated authors of the middle and upper social and economic strata. Letters, therefore, share with other written evidence the limitation of an imbalanced historical perspective. Furthermore, letters are interactive social documents. The author's perceptions of the recipient and the intended effect of a letter upon the recipient influence content, style, and language. Cultural restraints upon emotional display and dictates of social courtesy during the nineteenth century often inhibited honest expressions of tension or conflict in women's correspondence. In light of such limitations, analysis of letters for historical information requires careful evaluation of the author's motives, based on an understanding of her historical context, and consistent comparison with other available sources.

The letters written and received by Anna Wellington Stoner between 1873 and 1883 provide an excellent example of the kinds of historical information concealed in personal letters. From the time she first learned to compose letters, Anna followed her mother's advice to include not only descriptions of her mundane activities but also her emotional and intellectual reactions to life about her. Anna's letters reveal one woman's evolving self-concept from the time she was an adolescent and document her changing ideas about her multiple roles within her family and community. Anna Stoner lived almost a century, from 1857 to 1953, long enough to have a strong impact upon her descendants, acquaintances, and community. Corroboration of information in her letters is possible through public records, such as censuses, deeds, brand registrations, tax accounts, and probate minutes, as well as through extant family business records. Personal insights into Anna's character, personality, and values, all of which influenced her writing, are available through oral history interviews with three of her living grandchildren, who had almost daily contact with Anna during their formative years.

With few exceptions, Anna's letters to and from her mother, Martha Wellington, and her brother, Thomas, survived to the present, allowing the investigator to view their family relationships from multiple perspectives. To her mother, Anna was confidant, gossiping openly, sharing private jokes, and unabashedly boasting about her own children. A comparison of their earlier and later letters delineates the progressive change in mother-daughter roles, as Anna gradually matured in confidence and strength and her mother became more vulnerable and dependent. Close inspection of the attitudes of Anna and Martha discloses contradictions attributable to the differing ideologies of their two generations, while similarities between Martha's values and those of her daughter indicate the extent of her maternal influence. To Thomas Wellington, Anna was business adviser and personal motivator. Correspondence between brother and sister indicates clearly the progression of Thomas's fatal illness and some of its effects on his personality and relationships with his mother and sister. The optimistic outlook of her letters reflects Anna's energetic youthfulness but also exposes a sensitive bias toward her primary recipients. Through her positive images, Anna sought to reassure her mother and brother that she was not only willing but capable of assuming the responsibilities of adulthood. Unfortunately for historians, no Wellington-Stoner family letters composed during periods of mourning survived to the present. Likewise, if Anna recorded her thoughts and feelings about her courtship, wedding, confinements, and birthing experiences, those letters were sent beyond the close family circle and have not been saved. However, Anna's letters express candid feelings of frustration following financial reversals and insecurity when facing tough decisions. Her need to maintain close bonds with her mother and brother sometimes conflicted with the immediate needs of her husband and children.

The content of Anna's correspondence from the time she attended boarding school at the age of sixteen to her marriage at age twenty to when she was widowed at age twenty-seven parallels the progression of her maturing consciousness from self, to family, to social group. Like many newlywed rural women of her day, Anna's first years of marriage centered upon creating a home, bearing children, and struggling for daily survival, and her letters from those years focused upon the world of her own household. As she grew confident in her abilities to cope with the demands of her new role, Anna allowed her world to expand to include new experiences and new people. Born into a slaveholding household, Anna felt from birth the influence of Southern values and customs. In her relationships with other women, she was acutely aware of racial, economic, and cultural differences. Anna's writing reflects a condescending attitude toward persons of African and Mexican descent. On the other hand, she, like her mother, avoided women of her own race who considered themselves superior because of prestigious position or material wealth. Anna embraced the American ideals of femininity and domesticity, but expressed those ideals in a Western setting. Like other Texas women, her Southern romanticism was tempered by Western practicality. Almost joyfully, Anna abandoned the organized society of Victoria County, where tournaments and reunions celebrated the Lost Cause, and accepted the challenge of moving to the frontier of Southwest Texas, where wilderness conditions challenged former Confederates and Unionists alike. Experiencing unfamiliar sights and meeting new people almost daily provided Anna with many first impressions about which to write her closest relatives. Then, as Anna and her family became settled in their new environment, they also began extending themselves beyond their own household and kin to their community. In a time and place where families migrated often and with little notice, the Stoners became a stable element in community life.

Viewed through Anna's eyes, the story of the Stoner family's responses to transitions occurring in South Texas in the 1870s and 1880s contributes to an improved understanding of the everyday thoughts and feelings of nineteenth-century women, of the daily experiences of rural and frontier families, of evolving relationships among kin groups, and of social interactions between families. This is Anna's legacy, a treasure of personal memoirs reflecting the human side of history.

1
Write Often, Telling Everything

Refugio County
1852–1877

When Anna Louisa Wellington and William Clinton Stoner married in South Texas in November 1877, they faced together the challenge of establishing home and family in a period of rapid social and economic transition. For young Anna, this prospect was a familiar theme conveyed in the cherished correspondence of her maternal ancestors. In the opening years of the eighteenth century, when land grants first became available for purchase in the Virginia Piedmont, the Foster, Haskins, Ligon, Nash, and Williamson families migrated westward from the Tidewater, where their English and Welsh ancestors first broke the virgin soil of the New World. In western Virginia they cleared land and roads, founded churches and schools, and intermarried. A century later, the Piedmont was carved into as many cotton and corn plantations as the exhausted soil could support, and another generation joined the flow of migration westward. Into the trans-Appalachian frontier the migrants carried with them the plantation culture that was their heritage. As the physical distance between the generations grew and the chances of their being reunited lessened, letters became their primary means for maintaining family continuity.[1]

When Williamson Foster, his wife, Ann Haskins Ligon Foster, their six living children, and a few inherited slaves migrated westward from Prince Edward County, Virginia, during the winter of 1830–31, they followed the route of kin who had preceded them. By spring 1831, they reached Haywood County in western Tennessee, where Ann's brothers, William and Benjamin Ligon, settled earlier. Soon after the birth of their youngest child, the Fosters continued their journey westward, crossing the Mississippi River and entering Arkansas Territory. Their destination was the southwestern edge of the frontier along the Arkansas border with Mexican Texas. There the Fosters settled in Hempstead County near the Red River, where abundant water and fertile soil held great promise for cultivation.

The prosperity of Hempstead County attracted other families from Virginia, including relatives of the Fosters, and by 1836, when Arkansas attained statehood, the Red River and its tributaries were lined with the homes of planters, where antebellum gentility coexisted with the wilderness. Ann Foster's younger sister, Phoebe Haskins Ligon, and Phoebe's husband, Phineas Nash, established the second largest plantation in the county, with over fifty slaves. In the late 1830s, the village of Washington became a focal point where migrants moving into the new Republic of Texas stopped to gather supplies before crossing the Red River at Fulton. About fifteen miles south of Washington where the road leading to Louisiana touched Bois d'Arc Creek, Williamson Foster and his neighbors organized Spring Hill Female Academy to perpetuate for their daughters the values and customs of nineteenth-century domesticity. Under the instruction of Yankee schoolmistress Elizabeth Pratt, a pupil and disciple of renowned educator Emma Willard of Troy, New York, the Fosters' four daughters learned grammar, rhetoric, and composition. The girls practiced their skills in letters to their Virginia and Tennessee relatives.[2]

Martha Elizabeth, or "Betty," the Fosters' third daughter, born 14 August 1823 in Virginia, became the primary correspondent for the family following the deaths of her older sisters, Mary Jane and Cornelia Ann, and the marriage of her younger sister, Louisa Virginia, to Spring Hill merchant Chauncey Jones Harvey Betts. Increased responsibility fell upon Martha Elizabeth following the death of her father on 26 November 1848. Her brothers, George Williamson, Benjamin Haskins, and Patrick Henry, supervised the field hands while Martha managed the plantation household and cared for her widowed mother.[3]

Whenever a family member or slave was ill, Martha and her brothers sent for physician Royal Wetherton Wellington, a recent arrival in Hempstead County. Wellington, born 18 July 1815 and orphaned early in life, left his native Philadelphia in the late 1830s to seek a place of opportunity in the West. He served as an army doctor in St. Louis, practiced private medicine in Bolivar and Springfield, Missouri, and Hillsboro, Illinois, participated in freemasonry, and served as a bank director before reaching the bustling village of Fulton, Arkansas, in 1847.[4] Fulton served as a conduit for steady streams of migrants entering Texas, recently admitted to the union, and for companies of troops traveling southwestward during the Mexican War. While he traveled from village to village

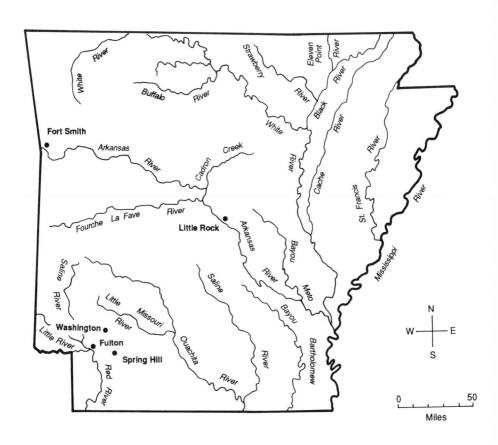

Arkansas, 1848. Detail of Hempstead County.

throughout Hempstead County, his saddle bag filled with medical implements and supplies, Wellington contemplated joining the throngs migrating into Texas. His close friend, Thomas Ruffin, a former circuit attorney in Missouri, visited Texas in the fall of 1849 and sent Wellington unfavorable reports of the soil, crops, and livestock. Corresponding from Richmond, Fort Bend County, Ruffin especially disdained the new state's climate, which fostered malaria in the coastal areas. For physicians, the potential of collecting high fees in Texas was offset, Ruffin claimed, by the fact that the doctors themselves "almost invariably get sick while sickness is prevailing, and . . . they have not made much here in the past season having been themselves sick a considerable portion of the time" [15 November 1849].[5]

During 1848–1850, as he considered his future, Royal Wellington frequently visited the Foster home, nestled deep in a pine forest between Fulton and Spring Hill. For the family's ailments, he provided tonics, cathartic pills, castor oil, and bitters. In addition, from his saddle-bag drug store, Wellington furnished ground cinnamon, ginger, and mustard for widow Ann Foster and hair oil for George. He treated Louisa V. Betts's children and prescribed bitter-tasting elixir of vitriol for Martha Elizabeth.[6] By the spring of 1850, the doctor had become attracted to the Southern way of life led by the Fosters and their neighbors and wrote Ruffin that he planned to leave the Red River area soon, forego his medical profession, and engage in planting. In reply, Ruffin encouraged Wellington to pursue his goal, but warned against settling in Texas:

> As for Texas I regret that I lived there so long as I did for all things considered I regard it as the most disagreeable country that I have ever visited, for its bad waters, hot and bilious climate more than counter balance any of its advantages. [28 April 1850]

On 3 August 1850, Ann Ligon Foster died, and her living sons and daughters divided her portion of Williamson Foster's estate as specified in his will. The eldest son, George, inherited a 560-acre tract of land; the younger sons, Benjamin and Patrick, received equal shares of Red River bottom land. Martha Elizabeth and her sister, Louisa V. Betts, together inherited one eighty-acre tract of timber and one four-hundred-acre tract of farmland, as well as an equal share with their brothers of the estate's slaves, livestock, cash, and other property.[7] An intelligent, educated Southern woman of twenty-seven, with land and slaves and experience in managing both, Martha Elizabeth Foster was an attractive marriage partner. Although he himself had few material assets—only his medical instruments, books, and pharmaceutical supplies—Royal Wellington, at the age of thirty-five, asked Martha to be his wife. Their wedding took place at the Foster plantation on 23 January 1851.[8]

The next June, accompanied by some slaves, Wellington left his bride and traveled into Texas to locate a promising site, in spite of his friend Ruffin's low opinion of the state. From Washington County, Texas, in July 1851, Royal announced his decision to Martha: "I intend to locate on or near the Gulf—this is certainly one of the best states in the Union and money is made more easily than any other country I have ever seen" [9 July 1851]. Upon his return to Arkansas in September, Wellington began collecting his patients' outstanding accounts and prepared to move to Texas.

Letters from Texas
1852–1860

In the spring of 1852, Martha Foster Wellington, pregnant with her first child, bade farewell to her brothers, sisters, aunts, and cousins in Arkansas and joined her doctor-husband on the long journey into South Texas. Her migration initiated the second generation of family letters from the West. Through their correspondence with their kin in Arkansas, the Wellingtons kept up with news of marriages, births, and deaths in the family and community, as well as the progress of crops and business dealings. The Foster brothers and sisters also exchanged greetings and news on behalf of their slaves, many of whom had suffered separation from their own families first when the Foster estate was divided and again when the Wellingtons moved to Texas.[9]

Traveling down the Red River to Shreveport, Louisiana, then overland southward toward the Texas coastal plain, the Wellingtons arrived at their destination in Indianola, a thriving seaport on Matagorda Bay that handled the bulk of the cotton exports for South Texas and served as the United States Army depot for Texas. With Martha and her household servants temporarily settled in rented rooms in Indianola, Wellington traveled throughout the coastal area investigating potential plantation sites. By late summer, the couple was living in the village of Saluria on Matagorda Island, where cool Gulf breezes made the hot, humid summer bearable. There, on 30 August 1852, Martha gave birth to a son, and Royal purchased a family Bible in which to record his son's impressive name, Thomas Ruffin Albert Wellington.[10]

The next winter, Martha and the baby lived in Port Lavaca while Wellington and Giles, a slave, looked for fertile farmland along the river bottoms, where heavy inland soil produced large quantities of cotton and corn, and on the prairie, where vast savannas provided forage for wild longhorns and mustangs. Along the south side of the San Antonio River, which delineated the boundary between Refugio and Victoria counties, and a few miles upstream from its point of convergence with the Guadalupe River, Wellington located one thousand acres. The land, a narrow rectangular strip, rising from a one-half-mile-wide river frontage to a rolling prairie three-and-a-half miles long, was originally part of the league granted to the seller Edward Perry by the Mexican government.[11] By the spring of 1854, the Wellingtons were living in their home on the San Antonio River and receiving mail at Anaqua, the nearest post office, accessible by ferry on the Victoria County side of the San Antonio River.[12]

With slave labor and occasional hired hands, Wellington worked hard to recover his land investment and create a large enough profit to purchase more slaves. Even though he had once planned to give up his medical practice, the needs of coastal residents demanded his services, and Wellington served as the primary doctor for an area extending from Goliad, twenty-five miles west of his farm, to Lamar, twenty miles southeastward on Aransas Bay. In addition to cotton and corn, he raised cattle, which ranged throughout Refugio County bearing his registered brand,⟨R⟩.[13]

In the summer of 1855, Martha Wellington returned to Arkansas with her young son to visit relatives for several months. They traveled by boat from Indianola to Galveston and then by steamboat to New Orleans, where they met C. J. H. Betts, who accompanied them up the Mississippi and Red rivers by shallow draft steamboat to Shreveport and, finally, by carriage to Spring Hill.[14] While in Arkansas, Martha received a letter from Royal informing her of the state of the crops and the welfare of their neighbors. He reported that one neighbor, Mrs. Fagan, wanted to return the slave Hannah, whom she had recently bought from Wellington and who refused to work for her new mistress. Wellington wrote Martha that he had advised Mrs. Fagan that all Hannah needed was a mistress with a whip. After he told Mrs. Fagan to caution Hannah that if he had to buy her back, he would whip her thoroughly, the slave went to work and caused no more complaints, Wellington claimed [7 August 1855]. Wellington's reputation as a strict disciplinarian earned him an appointment by the county court in November 1856 as captain of a slave patrol that scouted the area, especially at night, to prevent runaway slaves from

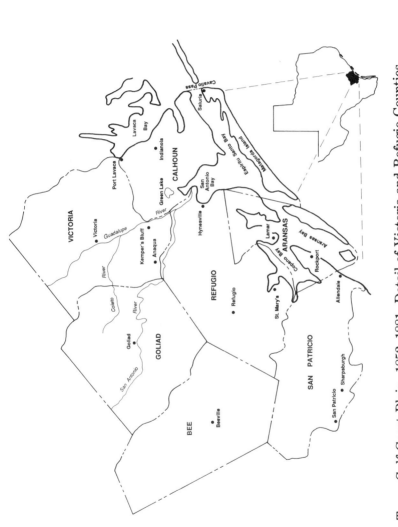

Texas Gulf Coast Plain, 1852–1881. Detail of Victoria and Refugio Counties.

crossing the San Antonio River and fleeing toward Mexico.[15] Since Wellington instructed a neighboring woman to discipline her slave with the whip, the possibility exists that he expected similar actions from his own wife, at least during his absences from their farm. Nonetheless, correspondence among Martha Wellington's Foster and Ligon relatives in Arkansas, Tennessee, and Virginia demonstrated warm affection for certain favored slaves that had been with the family through several generations. Letters during the 1850s and early 1860s contained moving messages from slaves in one household in one state to their mothers, sisters, brothers, and cousins in another.

As their land and cattle prospered, their slaves multiplied, and the doctor's medical practice grew, the Wellingtons' family also increased with the birth of a daughter on 17 January 1857. Martha named her child Anna Louisa after her mother and sister, but the family nicknamed her "Nannie," and hers became the second name listed in the family Bible. Announcements of Anna's birth to relatives back in Arkansas met with enthusiastic responses. In reply, Benjamin Haskins Foster teased Martha: "Your little girl must have taken her blue eyes from her grand papa She must have taken her beauty from her Uncle Ben, but not his badness" [13 April 1857]. Louisa V. Betts answered Martha's announcement with an expression of joy: "There was great rejoicing amongst us and I felt highly complimented at your putting Louisa to her name, but I hope that you will call her Anna for our Mama" [18 May 1857]. During Anna's early years, Royal Wellington proved himself a successful yeoman farmer with expectations of increased prosperity. His 1860 tax valuation for real estate, including 1008 acres of land, was $16,000, and for personal property, including eighteen slaves, nine horses, and seventy head of cattle, was $23,000. Only one farmer in Refugio County owned more slaves than Wellington in 1860. Wellington built seven houses on his farm to accommodate seven adult slaves (five women and two men, aged 21 to 50), and ten children (seven girls and three boys, aged 2 to 13).[16] Anna and Thomas's earliest playmates were probably these slave children.

Letters in the Storm
1861–1875

Events in the larger world quickly combined to change life forever for the Wellingtons and their neighbors. Letters to Anaqua from southwestern Arkansas throughout 1860 and 1861 alluded to strong secessionist sentiment among the Fosters, Bettses, and Nashes. Support for secession also ran high in Victoria and Refugio counties of Texas. Anticipating the outcome of the 23 February 1861 secession referendum, Ben McCulloch and his volunteer unit forced United States General D. E. Twiggs of the San Antonio garrison to sign evacuation orders for all federal troops. From Central and West Texas, federal forces marched toward Matagorda Bay to board ships at Indianola. While awaiting evacuation, the federal troops camped at Green Lake, in Calhoun County, less than ten miles east of Anaqua. When Fort Sumter fell in April 1861, Colonel Earl Van Dorn was detached to Texas to prevent the federal troops' departure. Blocking off Pass Cavallo, Van Dorn captured five hundred Union troops at Saluria.[17] With such dramatic events so near at hand, excitement over the war grew in Victoria and Refugio counties and men eagerly enlisted in the Confederate forces.

Although many of his acquaintances participated actively in Confederate military service, Royal Wellington continued practicing medicine and overseeing his farm during the Civil War. A home guard unit led by Wellington's neighbor and frequent patient, Peter Fagan, organized in 1861 to protect Refugio County residents along the San Antonio River. Whether or not Wellington participated in the home guard is unknown; its muster rolls no longer exist.[18] Many area physicians joined the Confederacy or devoted their practice to military troops in the area; at least one, Robert Bello, eventually was taken prisoner by federal troops at Indianola.[19] Wellington's services were, therefore, in great demand among the inhabitants of the area. His journal records his medical practice among the townspeople of Lamar in Aransas County and St. Mary's in Refugio County, as well as among rural stock raisers, farmers, planters, and slaves. Stock raisers called upon Wellington to treat their livestock, also, and his journal contains remedies for horse and cattle diseases. In exchange for medical treatment during the war years, Wellington often accepted salt, corn, flour, and beef in lieu of cash. Although he had assumed the role of slaveholder, served on the local slave patrol, and expressed sympathy for the Confederacy by feeding passing Confederate soldiers and their horses, Wellington contradicted his adoption of Southern culture by beginning the practice of paying annual wages to two slaves in December 1861. He hired John for fifty dollars a year and Lizzie for one hundred dollars a year. Perhaps he also freed them at that time. With their help, he delivered over eleven thousand pounds of cotton to Corpus Christi in May 1862.[20]

Confederate domination of Matagorda Bay was short-lived, and as the Civil War continued, hardship became a way of life for coastal residents. In 1862 Confederate forces in the Gulf of Mexico destroyed all lighthouses with the potential for guiding federal ships into the bays. At Saluria, the army evacuated residents, herded cattle to the mainland, and exploded the lighthouse, causing a fire that quickly engulfed the entire village. Saluria resident Elizabeth Mainland, the wife of John Mainland, captain of a Pass Cavallo pilot boat, and her nephew sought refuge at Anaqua with the Wellingtons. The Confederates' attempt to block federal invasion ultimately failed, and in November 1863, Union gunboats appeared in Matagorda Bay and quickly captured Indianola. Union forces eventually con-

trolled the Texas coast from Indianola southward to Browns-
ville.[21] Families along the Texas coast, cut off by the federal
blockade from the rest of the Confederacy, adapted to short-
ages by reclaiming the skills of previous generations. They
made their own cloth and tallow candles and substituted
parched corn, dried potatoes, or okra seeds for coffee. The only
substantial agriculture in Refugio County centered among the
San Antonio River farms, which continued to produce corn and
beef in spite of the labor shortage. Their goods fed the desti-
tute families of Refugio County soldiers and provided meals for
nearby troops.[22]

For the duration of the war, Royal Wellington's continued
medical practice and crop production contributed to the welfare
of his family and their neighbors. Letters received by Martha
Wellington during the war years alluded to the Wellington family's reported well-being, which contrasted with their correspondents' more difficult experiences. In the summer of 1861,
Louisa V. Betts sent Martha a glowing account of her family's
prosperous wheat and corn crops and encouraged the Wellingtons to return to Arkansas. Louisa claimed, "We have plenty
throughout the country and you need not be afraid of starving.
I mean plenty of bread and meat and potatoes" [13 August
1861]. In less than a year, however, the situation in Arkansas
changed, and Louisa then wrote her sister, "We were very glad
to hear that you were doing so well out where you live. I assure you that it is a great deal better than we are doing here"
[8 July 1862]. The year 1862 brought drought to Hempstead
County and the Betts family and their neighbors lost both food
and cash crops. Arkansas families, like all Southerners, began
to feel the effects of the loss of imported and manufactured
goods. Any merchandise of value, especially tea, coffee, and
calico, disappeared from Betts's store shelves. Concerning
clothing materials, Louisa wrote Martha:

> There is very little if any cloth in the stores throughout
> the country now. It has all been sold and very near all

mad[e] up and is now worn. There are families that have
no cloth to make up and not enough clothes for their children. . . . All the old looms have been fixed up and people
are trying to get some clothes mad[e] for their negroes
next winter, very few have given them any summer
clothes. [8 July 1862]

In 1864 Elizabeth Mainland and her husband returned to Matagorda Island and located shelter in a shack with only a partial
roof and fallen chimney. Because of his intimate knowledge of
Pass Cavallo, John Mainland was appointed by the Confederacy
to the dangerous task of piloting blockade runners. Although
Elizabeth Mainland wrote Martha Wellington that she felt obli-
gated toward her recent hostess for her "trouble and kindness,"
she found some irony in Martha's accounts of the Wellingtons'
relative comfort. Elizabeth wrote:

I was truly glad to hear from you and to hear that you
were all well and that things were looking so well. I am
glad the doctor had a good crop so that he can have something for his work and he can feed the soldiers and horses
when they come along. I am glad too that you have all
your goods. You don't care how long the cruel war lasts do
you. Yes you do. I know you care for the dear men. [4
November 1864]

The threat of raids from federal vessels in coastal waters
near Refugio County inhibited social gatherings and confined
women and children to their homes. Martha Wellington continued her housework and maintained her pastime of letter writing, although mail delivery was slow and uncertain. She also
assumed the role of teacher for her young children. Prior to the
war, Thomas attended Lamar Academy, a private school conducted by Jane P. O'Connor in the village of Lamar on Aransas
Bay. Several children of the Refugio County farmers and stock

raisers whose land bordered the San Antonio River attended the academy and boarded with village families.[23] With private schools closed during the war, however, Martha herself taught her children. She attempted to teach Anna fancy stitchery, encouraging the young child to complete an alphabet sampler she and her sisters had begun when they were young, but Anna was not interested in fine sewing. The Wellington household contained several books in addition to medical guides and the Bible, such as works on Christian doctrine and household management, and the Wellingtons encouraged their children to develop good reading skills from an early age.

Following the Civil War, Reconstruction brought a decade of increased economic hardship to the Wellingtons and their neighbors, who found themselves without the labor supply to continue large-scale production on their land. Following emancipation, Royal Wellington attempted to maintain his farm's income by increasing his productive acreage and hiring laborers from among former slaves and from the Mexican-American population. In January 1866, he leased an additional 150 acres of land on the San Antonio River. He hired two former house servants, Betsy and Lizzie, providing them small wages and some clothing. During 1867 and 1868, he hired Billy Rice, a freedman, to oversee laborers working corn and cotton crops and splitting rails for fencing.[24] In spite of his efforts, Wellington's income from cotton in 1868 was only $126. Reconstruction taxes added to Wellington's hardship, including quarterly occupation taxes and property taxes, levied under such various forms as United States direct taxes, special revenue taxes, internal revenue taxes, frontier defense taxes, and public school taxes.[25]

Such economic hardships, combined with the unhealthy climate of the coast, caused Wellington to investigate alternative places to settle his family. During 1866–67, when yellow fever raged throughout the lowland counties, he contemplated emigrating either to Mexico or to the reportedly healthy environs of the bay islands of Honduras. When Martha wrote her Aunt Phoebe Nash about the doctor's plans, Phoebe answered with regret that the Wellingtons might join the colonies of emigrants forming throughout the former Confederacy. Equating the will of God with that of a husband, the aging aunt reminded Martha of her duty as a submissive wife:

> Where our husbands take us are often matters we cant controll we have all to settle down quietly and enjoy a life of labour. But our ways are not God's ways and we know all things worke together for good to those who love and serve God. [10 October 1866]

Instead of emigrating, Wellington rented out the farm, house, and 150 acres of leased land, and moved his family in March 1868 into Victoria, where his children attended re-opened private schools. The lessee, Elijah Dickrow, failed to pay the rent, however, and on 10 February 1869, Wellington accepted a lien on Dickrow's livestock to secure the overdue rent of $515.[26] By summer 1870, the Wellington family had returned to their home on the San Antonio River, and when the ninth United States Census was gathered that July, Royal Wellington reported owning real estate worth only $3,000 and personal property worth $500, a substantial decrease since 1860, when he had reported assets valued at $39,000.[27]

Anna Louisa Wellington was five years old when the Civil War began and eighteen when Reconstruction ended. She undoubtedly learned much in her formative years about making do and doing without, lessons that would serve her well later in life. Seventy-three years later, Anna recalled the following verse of a hymn learned from her mother during those difficult years of war and Reconstruction:

> I would not live alway, I ask not to stay,
> Where storm after storm rises dark on the way—

The few lucid moments that dawn on us here
Are enough for life's triumphs, full enough for life's
cheer.[28]

Letters as Lessons
1873–1877

In spite of increasing financial difficulties during Reconstruction, Royal and Martha Wellington gave priority to their children's education. Anna and Thomas's early training at home prepared them well for formal academic training. Public schools had not yet opened in Victoria or Refugio counties, but private academies furnished primary and secondary education for those students whose families could afford to pay tuition. When the Wellingtons moved into Victoria in 1868 for a brief period, they enrolled eleven-year-old Anna in the Victoria Female Academy. Founded twenty years earlier by Presbyterian minister John R. Shive and his wife, Viola H. Shive, Victoria Female Academy was one of Texas's leading nineteenth-century educational institutions. The school had literary, classical, music, and art departments, and offered advanced mathematics, including trigonometry and calculus, and sciences, including botany and astronomy. Following the death of John Shive in 1853, Viola Shive continued to operate the school with the aid of Joel T. Case, pastor of Victoria's First Presbyterian Church. In 1858 the city of Victoria erected a large building to house the academy, but four years later Viola Shive married Reverend Case and the couple moved to Clinton, DeWitt County, to pastor the Presbyterian church there. Following the Civil War, the Cases returned to Victoria to reopen the academy. The year 1868, when Anna first enrolled, was a difficult one for the school. Under the financial strains of Reconstruction, the city failed to complete payments on the school building and was forced to sell it. Then, in June of that year,

Joel Case died. Professor C. Reisner, director of the school's fine arts program, bought the property from the city and leased it to Viola Case for a brief time. In 1869, the academy became coeducational, one of the first schools in Texas to do so, and Thomas Wellington became one of the school's first male pupils. In 1870, Viola Case moved the school into her home and changed its name to Mrs. Case's Select School.[29] During that year of transition for the Case School, Anna and Thomas Wellington attended the school of James L. Witkins. Their father paid part of their tuition with $50 cash and received $2.50 credit from Witkins for a pair of shoes, leaving a balance of $22.50. The tuition covered two periods, from 3 January to 31 July and from 26 September to 14 October 1870.[30]

During their school years, Thomas and Anna shared the textbook, *Willard's School History of the United States*, published in 1866 by the same Emma Willard whose disciple had taught their mother at Spring Hill Academy in Arkansas.[31] In Victoria, Anna became friends with some of the daughters of the area's most privileged families. Along with her friends, she received an invitation to the Coronation Ball of the first tournament in Victoria, held on 19 August 1869. The Victoria tournaments, modeled upon the feudal games of Elizabethan England, provided an outlet for the frustrated energies of former Confederate soldiers, who organized the equestrian sporting events and the elaborate coronation of the Queen of Love and Beauty, chosen for the honor by the tournament winner. Shy by nature, twelve-year-old Anna declined the tournament invitation. Encouraged by her mother to remain reserved socially, Anna also avoided other public events.[32]

After 1870, when Martha and Royal Wellington returned to their San Antonio River farm, their children boarded in Victoria during school sessions. Their absence provided Martha the opportunity to pass on to her children the family tradition of letter writing. Deliberately and systematically, she instructed Anna and Thomas in effective correspondence, and along with the technique of writing fully detailed letters, she taught them lessons in morality and gender roles. Anna received subtle instruction in domesticity through her mother's careful recounting of the mundane activities that were part of her daily contributions to the Wellington farm: feeding poultry, gathering eggs, overseeing the garden, churning, sewing, washing, and occasionally visiting neighbors. In letters to Thomas, Martha reported news concerning family business affairs, such as income from sales of cattle or payments of patients' accounts, and made requests of Thomas to sell eggs and butter in town. Her primary purpose in writing her son, however, was to fulfill her duty as guardian of his moral character in spite of the distance separating them. Like other nineteenth-century parents, the Wellingtons created tension for their adolescent children by allowing them to live apart from the family and yet expecting the separation to yield stronger family bonds. Letters, then, became more than information exchanges; they were the vehicles for instruction in family duty and loyalty.[33]

On Thursday, 10 April 1873, Martha Wellington began a letter to her children that she sent to them a week later with friends from Victoria returning from a visit in the Anaqua area. With her letter, Martha sent both children gifts and money from home. A while before, with the help of neighbors going to town, she had sent them $5.50 cash, with which Thomas was to procure for his sister a month's tuition for music lessons. "I wish you to *do* so," she wrote Anna, referring to the lessons, and added, "If your Bro. can find you a musick teacher out of the convent I would prefer it—If not take them there."[34] Both Anna and Thomas were in Case School, but only Thomas boarded there. Anna lived in Victoria with family friends, and her mother encouraged her to move to the school after the end of the month. "If you can get a room at Mrs. Case's I would rather you both boarded at the same place," Martha wrote, "so that you can be together more & give each other some assistance." One reason Martha thought Anna should move was that she had not let her mother know how she felt about her living arrangements. Martha insisted that her children withhold nothing from her, but share with her all their activities and thoughts:

> In your letters I hope that you both will tell me every-thing that happens to you without reserve—To do so you would have to write at leisure or keep a kind of diary & every night write what has happened to you during the day & send it to me finished in a letter form.

Continuing her letter the next day, Martha began by telling her children that Mr. Clancey, a neighbor, had just brought much-welcomed news from them, and in her gratitude, she exclaimed, "Our friends are very kind to offer to bring us news of your wellfare & carry any thing we wish to send you. You have no idea how much we have missed you." Then, she returned to the lesson in letter writing she had started the previous day and emphatically admonished the two children about the inter-relation of skillful writing and family duty:

> We are glad to hear you are well & in good spirits—I wish that I could know that you are improving fast expecially in letter writing—There is no *need* of your spelling wrong as I have often told you to *keep a Dictionary* by you & if you have none, *buy* one—This is why I wish you to write when you have plenty of time & only *conclude* in haste. *Study hard* and *my dear children try always to deserve the love, esteem and good opinion* of your parents and friends.

Proper grammar and spelling were important to Martha, but content rich in details is what she craved from her children's letters:

> You did not tell me if you attend church regular or not or about new things you have bought or whether you have had your picture taken. . . . I write *now* because no one

30

but a *mother* can tell what she would *wish* to say to her *only children*—You must consider it addressed to both of you & read it carefully and alone—And I do hope you will proffit by my advise—I would like to know what *books* you read—try and select something good and well recommended—Buy each of you a *Bible* & read it every night before you ly down.

To her twenty-one-year-old son, she added additional advice: "Tho[mas] my dear son I do hope and trust you will keep out of all houses of temptation to do wrong and spend your spare time in reading and improving your mind" [10 April 1873].

The response written by Anna and Thomas in answer to their mother's letter of 10 April 1873 has been lost, but when Martha wrote her son later, on 1 May, she mentioned that a neighbor had brought her a letter from them both written by Thomas. While both parents had welcomed news from their children, Thomas's letter had upset them. Martha explained the reason for their disappointment in the following way:

You may be sure when I saw the first part of your letter I thought it the *hight* of nonsense for though I was glad to hear from you I was sorry to know that you had not taken my advice & let the girls alone—I think your sister and myself have a right to complain if you neglected her to take some pretty school miss home at night—And I think you and her—the young miss I mean— both ought to have been thinking about your lessons instead of keeping each other company—But you were so candid with me to tell me of it & I must not scold you much.

Having spent much emotion on Thomas's moral correction, Martha proceeded to criticize his handwriting, grammar, and spelling. She warned him against using "certain inelligant expressions such as 'you bet', 'a jolly old time', 'go, or bust', 'break his neck,'" and she claimed she "couldn't find a-i-n-t in the dictionary." Such things as legible handwriting and correct spelling were important in letters, she believed, not only for clear communication, but because they reflected well on one's character. She admonished Thomas:

> Do not forget who is writing to you and who it is that feels the *deepest interest* in the welfare of her only children—I would not willingly hurt your feelings but it is your *improvement* that I desire *above all things* and feel it's my duty to correct your *'errors* of youth.' [1 May 1873]

Two weeks later, on Thursday, 15 May 1873, sixteen-year-old Anna composed her earliest extant letter to her mother, whom she addressed as "Dear Mama." In a self-conscious attempt to please her parents, she began by apologizing for writing with a lead pencil rather than with her pen, which had broken. Following her mother's advice, Anna reported her daily activities. The previous day she studied her Sunday School lesson in a Methodist class taught by Mrs. Heaton and tried unsuccessfully to cut a pattern of her overshirt. Earlier that week, Thomas took her to an evening show at the Masonic hall. "I cannot tell you what I saw now," Anna reported, "but I think it was worth my money he wanted me to go last night but I did not want to go so he said he would not go." Thanking her mother for the $5.50 she had sent in April and the extra $7.00 sent to town later with a neighbor, Anna reported the following purchases: a pair of cuff buttons, two yards of ribbon, and a money purse. She had acquired the services of Professor Reisner for piano lessons and claimed, "Mr. R thinks I am learning musick rite fast, I think he will give me the Herekoviene (I believe that is the way to spell it) for the next lesson I like musick so much." Anna intended to use the remaining money to have her picture taken and buy a pair of shoes. Seeking reassurance from her parents, Anna added that she hoped she and Thomas did not spend their money "extravagantly" [15 May 1873].

With her letter, Anna enclosed a half sheet of paper and an envelope for her mother's use in replying. Instead, Martha Wellington used one side of the clean sheet to enclose a letter to Thomas and wrote notes to her daughter in pen between the penciled lines of Anna's letter itself, thus enabling her to respond directly to each of Anna's statements and to correct her spelling and grammar. Martha began her reply on Thursday, 21 May 1873, and added to it the following day. Writing from Wellington, Martha began by telling Anna that "Papa" received the letter while he was riding the ferry across the river upon his return from the Bluffs and handed it to her as she put his supper on the table.[35] "He said it was written with such *pale ink* he could not read it," Martha wrote, teasing Anna about writing in pencil. Martha went on to explain the method she would use to answer Anna's letter:

> But he [Papa] spoiled the envelope so I cannot use it and I will spoil this page by interlining it & answering questions since you like that way of answering letters—I am going to correct bad spelling, too—Try and get a good pen and write with it next time though it was well it was written with pencil this time—you know why.

Martha then commented on Anna's letter, line by line. To the news that Anna had received some religious instruction, Martha replied, "I am glad to hear you are going to Sunday school and that you are interested in it also." Emotionally, she added, "I hope my prayers will be answered for my child yet—I count every day & week that is past as bringing the time for your return that much nearer—I am *so anxious* to see you but would not have you leave school till the session is out." Upon hearing that Anna had turned down Thomas's invitation to attend a second Masonic hall program, she responded, "You were right—do not go to such places too often—He was right for not going when you did not wish to go." Assuring Anna that she had spent her money wisely, Martha explained that she had just realized that lack of money was the reason Anna had not yet had her picture taken as requested earlier by her parents. Martha tied the misunderstanding to a lesson in femininity in the following manner:

> I did not know before why you did not have your picture taken—Your Bro. said it was because you were too bashful—He has got to learn that 'Modesty is a quality that highly adorns a lady'—I would much rather have you too modest than too bold.

Above the words *rite fast*, which Anna had used to describe her music teacher's reaction to her progress, Martha wrote, "*very* would sound better." To Anna's reference to her uncertainty about the spelling of the name of her new piano lesson, Martha admitted, "I have forgotten [the spelling] it has been so long since I have seen the piece of music." Anna's love of music met with Martha's firm approval, but she did not want her daughter's accomplishment to set her too far apart from her neighbors. Martha wrote, "I am pleased to hear you are fond of practicing (and by the way it is just 4 o'clock now & you are at the piano)—The Down's asked me if you were taking lessons but I gave them no satisfaction & no one else about here suspicions it." Thanking Anna for sending her some stamps earlier, Martha Wellington asked her daughter to send next a blouse pattern for her friends, adding that "the girls out here in the country are very much afraid you will get ahead of them in fashions." Martha closed her notes to Anna by writing, "I need not say take care of my letters & write soon to your affectionate mother." Along with lessons in domesticity and femininity, Martha taught Anna the significance of their correspondence. These were letters to take seriously, to read and reread, and, above all, to cherish.

When Martha continued her letter the next day, 22 May 1873, she wrote from Fair View, the farm of the Alexander Hawkins Cromwell family near Anaqua. Having filled all the clean spaces of Anna's letter, back and front, with her comments and suggestions, Martha began writing on the remaining blank pages of the stationery. Concerned that her markings would be illegible, Martha explained, "In reading over what I wrote yesterday I am afraid you will be more puzzled than [indecipherable] . . . I thought I would write something intelligible on this page." The news from Fair View was that the Cromwells were planning to hire their niece, Maria Stoner, to conduct school in their home for their daughter Nannie and for her friend Lillie, who would board with them. The girls would be good company for Nancy Michael Stoner Cromwell, Martha claimed, who was "very low spirited" about her daughter Lee's health. Concerning schools in their neighborhood, she wrote Anna:

> Every person seems anxious to start a school on this side
> of the river but no one is willing to take the lead and raise
> the money to build a house—I think it could be done if
> they would try—Several of our friends have asked me if
> we would take you home and send [you] to school from
> here if they make up one—I tell them I would rather you
> would remain in Victoria—You know why.

Martha did not elaborate immediately on the reason that she wished Anna to remain in school in Victoria, but turned to the subject of Anna's schoolmates there. "You have never writen me a word about your former associates," she scolded mildly. "Is Lizzy January in the Convent now? Have you never seen Bessie Mitchell, May Thomson, & Annie Hill? Are they going to school now? In your next tell me something about the people we used to know in town."

Next, Martha turned over the page and directed her attention toward Thomas, whom she teased tenderly as follows:

> I must try and not scold you this time & would not have
> done so before if I had known your 'heart' was already

'*broke*'—What a naughty *girl* she was to show you the 'bottom of her foot' at the ball—Was she dancing the '*heel & toe Polka*'? I'm sorry I have bad *news* for you, but your old S—H— [Martha inserted the word *sugar* over the line after the *S* and drew a heart above the line following the *H*] is *married* at the Bay—You have not forgotten Miss Vance have you? She is Mrs. Morgan now—Miss Kate Givens is also married to Dr. Clarke, formerly of Goliad now living at Rock Port.

Before telling Thomas about some cattle sales his father had made to Thomas O'Connor and asking her son to sell some butter and eggs for her in town, Martha shared more gossip with him, this time containing subtle advice against flirtatious girls and their mothers, as follows:

I heard that *little Jany Townsend* wanted to marry someone but her Papa & Mama *objected*, so they are having some trouble—Miss Jany sayes her mama *pushed her* forward & Mrs. T says if she had *another* girl to raise she would raise her very *differently*—So you see, *mothers* who push their children forward before they are grown are often compelled to sit on the 'stool of repentance' when it is *too late*—Do not *speak* of this to any one till you hear it some other way. [21 May 1873]

On Tuesday, 3 June 1873, writing again from Fair View, Martha Wellington wrote Anna and Thomas each one side, back and front, of a single sheet of paper. First, to Thomas she wrote that she would send a crock of fresh butter to sell and that he could keep the proceeds to use as he pleased. Martha planned to send the butter with hands taking corn to the mill. After several days of rain, the San Antonio River was on a rise, Martha wrote, but she hoped that Clayton, the ferryman, would be able to "set them over" soon so that Thomas could get the butter and so that she could hear from her children again.

With her letter to Thomas, Martha sent Anna four dollars, which, she said, was all the money she had. She also told Thomas she had hired William, the son of her former slave Betsy, and paid him for his work in food and clothes. "He is a great deal of help to me," Martha wrote. "He seems well satisfied & quick to do all we tell him to do."

On the opposite side of the paper, on the "same date a little later," Martha completed for Anna her thoughts concerning the reason she and Anna's father wanted their daughter to attend boarding school in Victoria rather than study with a tutor at a neighbor's ranch near home:

> I wish to tell you why your papa sent you to Victoria to school—He told me to-day it was to learn you how to behave—in other words to make a *lady* of you or that being among strangers you might acquire lady like manner—So I hope in *that* respect we will not be disappointed in your improvement and that you will *not* be the very '*same old Nan*' but more *dignified-polite* and at your *ease*—even if you have to *assume* such *manners* for you can *practice* them till they have become *natural* to you.

One aspect of femininity that Martha desired to inculcate in Anna was the proper balance between intimacy and reserve in her relationships with others. Martha advised Anna, "Do not seclude yourself too much from society but go into decent company every opportunity—Learn to be *polite* to all but not *too familiar* with *any*." Reiterating her earlier expectations for her daughter's improvement, Martha stated, "You are at an age now to form your character for *life* & every one will *expect* to see a *change* for the better in you on your return home—So do not even wish to be *exactly* the *same* that you were when you left" [3 June 1873].

The series of five letters between Martha Wellington and her children from 10 April to 3 June 1873 are the only extant evidence of their correspondence from the time Thomas and Anna began school in Victoria in 1868 to the spring of 1875, when Royal Wellington died. Undoubtedly, the combined lifestyle of farmer and country doctor frequently exposed Wellington to potential accidents and extreme weather conditions, as well as to infectious diseases. In the few letters Martha wrote Anna and Thomas in the single month of May 1873, she mentioned two succeeding cases of illness suffered by their father. During the last week of April, he was bitten by a poisonous spider, and Martha and their hired help, along with several neighbors, all tried to relieve his pain. Martha and her helpers forced him to drink "nearly a quart of pure whiskey" and rubbed his body with a whole bottle of pain killer. Finally, they administered morphine and "cupped him in five places" [1 May 1873]. Within two weeks of that experience, Wellington contracted a cold when he was caught in a rain shower on his way to Kemper's Bluff to get medicine. Perhaps as the result of similar circumstances, Royal Wellington died on 26 March 1875, at the age of fifty-nine years, and was buried the next day, presumably on his farm on the San Antonio River in Refugio County. Wellington's death may have been unforeseen; he died intestate. On 16 April 1875, an inventory of his estate resulted in an appraisal amounting to $7,609, based on property which included 1004 acres in Refugio County, eight horses, three mules, four hundred head of cattle, five oxen, a wagon, farming utensils, blacksmith tools, mill stones, and $842 in outstanding notes and accounts. On the same day, Martha made bond as administrator of her husband's estate; Thomas, however, actually managed the estate's legal and financial business, keeping a journal of all transactions. Recognizing changes taking place in Refugio County in the mid-1870s that were transforming the area's economic base from farming to ranching, Thomas tried various approaches to achieve success in the stock business. In the summer of 1875 he registered the Royal W. Wellington estate brand, ꓤ⅃, in Refugio, Victoria, and Aransas counties.[36]

No extant letters exist written between Martha, Anna, and Thomas Wellington during their period of mourning following the doctor's death. For the remainder of 1875, only four letters received by the Wellingtons survived, two each from Louisa V. Betts and S. Lindsley, a former friend of Royal Wellington. Both correspondents expressed alarm over not hearing from the family recently. Martha apparently postponed informing her sister and others of her husband's death for several months. By the time of his father's death, Thomas had ended his formal education and returned home to live. Most likely, Anna also remained at home through the summer following Wellington's death. When the fall term began, Anna continued studying at Case's academy. In December 1875, she wrote one last letter from school, asking anxiously why she had received no word from home in a long time. Also, Anna reminded her mother, "Be sure and send someone for me before Christmas. I want to get home & be quiet for awhile" [12 December 1875].

After Christmas 1875, Anna Wellington, now almost nineteen years of age, chose to end her educational career and remain at home. Her family's adjustment to the death of Royal Wellington coincided with a series of personal illnesses. In the early months of 1876, both Anna and Thomas contracted measles, and although Anna recovered completely, Thomas struggled with successive illnesses for the remainder of his life. In April 1876, Anna accompanied her mother and brother to Hempstead County, Arkansas, where she met for the first time members of the Foster, Betts, and Nash families, whom she had previously known only through correspondence. She visited, among others, her mother's cousin, Martha E. "Pattie" Nash Flanagin, whose husband, Harris Flanagin, served as the Confederate governor of Arkansas and later founded the town of Arkadelphia.[37] Pattie's mother, Martha's Aunt Phoebe Nash, was eighty-three years old when the Wellingtons visited Arkadelphia, but still she rode a mule from her farm outside town to see her niece and grand-niece from Texas.[38] All of Anna's maternal uncles—George, Benjamin, and Patrick Foster, and C. J. H. Betts—had died by the time of her Arkansas visit. Her aunt Louisa V. Betts encouraged the Wellingtons to return to Arkansas to join her family of nine children in the newly established county seat of Hope. Royal Wellington's estate remained unsettled, however, and Thomas returned to Refugio County in June to administer the family's business there.

Anna and Martha remained in Arkansas until the next fall. While there, Anna especially enjoyed the companionship of her cousin, Augusta Betts, who was just three years younger than she. Upon her return to Texas, Anna corresponded regularly with "Gusta," whose letters reflected the interests of many nineteenth-century young women: family and chores, church and school, social gatherings and beaus. Courtship and marriage were frequent topics of correspondence between the two. In March 1877, Augusta summarized their dilemma, writing Anna:

> Cousin Annie, you advised me to get married. . . . Is it so nice to be married? I believe I'll take the first opportunity that presents itself and make the experiment. Is that advisable to take the *first* whether I like him or not or must I wait for the one I *care for really* to present himself. But suppose the only one I care a snap of my finger for shouldn't present himself Oh! most horrible thought! [29 March 1877]

After leaving school in Victoria, Anna's social circle included only her familiar, rural neighbors along the San Antonio River near Anaqua, where a small store and post office served as the community's center. Anaqua had no organized church, but occasionally Presbyterian minister W. E. Caldwell from Goliad held services in area residences, including the Wellingtons' home. The Wellingtons' neighbors, Alexander Hawkins Cromwell, his wife Nancy, and their children, probably visited often with Martha, Thomas, and Anna when the minister held services. When Alexander Cromwell died around 1877, Martha, herself a recent widow, was probably a helpful companion to Nancy. On 25 July 1877, Caldwell performed the marriage of Nannie L. Cromwell and William B. Holliday in the Cromwells' home. Undoubtedly, Nannie's wedding was an important social event for her dearest friend, Anna Wellington. Then, just three months later, on 17 October 1877, Anna's friend, Lillie Blanche Rose, married Nannie's brother, Francis Hawkins Cromwell at the Cromwell home.[39]

The two Cromwell weddings only a few months apart afforded Anna opportunities to become acquainted with the Cromwells' visiting cousin, William Clinton Stoner. Born near Mt. Sterling, Kentucky, in 1852, Clinton Stoner was the eldest child of Thomas Chilton Stoner and Nancy Jane Hathaway Stoner, who had married in Montgomery County, Kentucky, on 3 September 1851. Thomas Chilton Stoner, born 24 March 1829, was a cousin of Nancy Michael Stoner Cromwell. The Cromwells left Kentucky in the 1850s and settled near Anaqua, where they farmed and operated a ferry. When the Cromwells migrated to Texas, they accompanied the family of Michael Lowery Stoner, the older brother of Thomas Chilton Stoner. Michael L. Stoner established the plantation Bleak Hill near the town of Victoria and later operated a hide and tallow plant at St. Mary's in Refugio County. During the Civil War, he served under Alfred M. Hobby in the Eighth Texas Infantry Battalion, which defended Corpus Christi, Matagorda Bay, Mustang Island, and St. Joseph's Island. In the winter of 1863, Stoner was captured and imprisoned at New Orleans, where he developed a cancerous growth on his lip that eventually became fatal. After his death in 1875, Michael L. Stoner's seven sons and daughters and their spouses organized the Stoner Pasture Company, a ranching enterprise, near Kemper's Bluff and appointed their eldest brother, George Overton Stoner, general manager.[40] About the same time his cousin and brother left Kentucky for Texas, Thomas Chilton Stoner moved his wife and young children from Kentucky to the prairies of central Illinois. When the Civil War began, however, the family retreated to his parents' home in Mt. Sterling. Thomas Stoner joined the Confederate troops while his family remained with his father. Some of the Stoners that had moved to Texas also retreated to their homeplace in Kentucky. As the war progressed, the Stoner elders, women, and children fled through the mountains of eastern Kentucky to refuge in Virginia. Following the war, Thomas C. and Nancy Stoner returned to Illinois and settled near Mt. Zion in Macon County. They took with them four children: William Clinton, Mary Petetta, Thomas Chilton, Jr., and Robert Lee. In Illinois, two more Stoner children, Nancy and Mattie Allen, were born. Thomas C. Stoner inherited a penchant for hunting, fishing, and horse racing from his ancestor, George Michael Stoner, Daniel Boone's companion, and while his sons managed the mundane farm work, he enjoyed fishing expeditions and fox hunts.[41] His eldest son, William Clinton, differed from Stoner in temperament and, upon reaching his early twenties, decided to escape his father's dominance and seek his own, separate future among his Texas kin.

Since Clinton Stoner's experience was with crops rather than cattle, he probably felt more at home on the Cromwell family farm than with his cousins who ran the Stoner Pasture Company.[42] While living with the Cromwells at their farm, Fair View, near Anaqua, he met Anna Louisa Wellington. Besides being the Cromwells' neighbor, Anna had known the daughters and daughters-in-law of Clinton's uncle, Michael L. Stoner, during her school years in Victoria. On Wednesday, 28 November 1877, W. E. Caldwell performed still another wedding in the Anaqua neighborhood when Anna Louisa Wellington married William Clinton Stoner at her mother's home.[43] Anna was soon to inherit one-fourth of her father's

Marriage License, Anna Louisa Wellington and William Clinton Stoner, 28 November 1877. Reproduced by permission of The Texas Collection, Baylor University, Waco, Texas.

land, and Clinton set about to rejuvenate the fields of the old Wellington farm.

* * * * *

Like their ancestors before them, Anna and Clinton Stoner began married life in a time of economic and social upheaval. In a majority of cases, the parents of the generation of South Texans that came into adulthood in the 1870s consisted of original colonists or later settlers who immigrated from other Southern states during the 1840s and 1850s. By applying plantation economics to their new environment, a few achieved planter status and many became prosperous yeoman farmers. The failure of the Confederacy stripped the fortunes of the parents but not the ambition of the children. Holding fast to the belief that with courage, intelligence, and patience they could rebuild their families' fortunes, newly married couples endured inconveniences and continuous hard work in order to obtain a measure of the American dream, which in Texas meant owning land, cattle, buildings, and cash. Like generations before them, many young couples discovered that the ways of their parents no longer worked in a transformed economy and faced the challenge of discovering new methods of making a living. Maintaining continuity with their extended families while establishing their separate identity as a family unit was important to Anna and Clinton Stoner. Encouraged by the examples preserved by Anna's parents and grandparents in their correspondence, the Stoners accepted their own role in the continuation of the family legacy.

2
A Smiling Providence

Victoria County
November 1877–September 1881

Following the Civil War, large-scale cotton production ceased and cattle replaced cotton as the primary product of the coastal plains of South Texas. In 1870 most rural families in both Victoria and Refugio counties operated farms and owned small to medium-sized cattle herds which grazed the open range. Ten years later, with the diminishment of cattle drives and the introduction of barbed wire fencing, only a few wealthy ranchers owned most of the land. Rail fences, such as that begun by Royal Wellington in 1867 to enclose pastures on land along the San Antonio River, required expensive materials and labor, took years to complete, and were unsatisfactory barriers

45

for the longhorns and mustangs that thrived on South Texas prairies. In 1870, Thomas O'Connor, a neighbor of the Wellington family, built an extensive plank fence enclosing almost the entire eastern half of Refugio County from the San Antonio River to Mission River to Copano Bay. Then, in 1876, O'Connor began replacing his planks with inexpensive and effective barbed wire. In Victoria County, George Overton Stoner, Clinton Stoner's cousin and manager of the Stoner Pasture Company, enclosed about twenty thousand acres from Clark's Point eastward along the southern side of the Guadalupe River to Kemper's Bluff. James A. McFaddin built a barbed wire enclosure for thirty thousand acres of land, extending southeastward from Kemper's Bluff to the fork of the Guadalupe and San Antonio rivers.[1] Other cattlemen who had concentrated on buying land at depressed prices also enclosed their holdings and required the removal of all cattle bearing brands other than their own, forcing out of business those farmer–stock raisers who had invested in cattle, not land. Even if they owned enough land to maintain profitable herds, many stock raisers discovered that the fences of the ranchers cut off access to natural watering places. Left with insufficient pasturage and water for their cattle, most cattle raisers in the low country sold their herds and land to the ranchers and faced three choices: assume jobs on the large ranches, move into town to enter a trade or profession, or join the movement toward the western frontier, where affordable land was available and the range remained free.

As fencing pushed middle-class farm families off the land, rural community life in Refugio and Victoria counties disappeared. Small schools, local stores, and post offices closed. The sense of community, which had formerly centered around rural neighborhoods, dispersed over a wider area and gradually dissolved. Fencing brought an end to a way of life for many South Texans. In 1877 Thomas Wellington reported to his father's former correspondent, S. Lindsley, a retired Refugio County school teacher who had moved to Ohio, that the country had become crisscrossed with fences. Lindsley responded to Thomas's letter poignantly, recalling with fondness his former home on "the green open prairy, bounded only by the horizon, whilst thousands of horses and cattle roamed unrestrained over it" [6 August 1877].

Adapting to economic and social changes taking place in South Texas was particularly challenging to newly married couples such as Anna and Clinton Stoner. From 1878 to 1881, while the Stoners set up separate housekeeping and established their individual roles within their family, letter writing served as the young bride's primary outlet for expressing her thoughts and feelings about her new life in a changing environment. The major themes of Anna's letters were the problems that arose in the daily routine of farm work and housekeeping and the solutions she and Clinton found and created to cope with those problems. Also, a regular part of every letter Anna wrote was a report on the health of her family and neighbors. A farm wife's role required creativity and intelligence to stretch the family's limited resources. As her letters reveal, Anna approached her task with the youthful conviction that most difficulties were only temporary inconveniences and that with enough hard work and perseverance, times would improve. As she found innovative solutions to smaller problems, Anna's confidence in her ability to cope with larger issues grew.

Twenty-seven letters written by Anna Stoner to her mother, Martha, and one letter to her brother, Thomas, from the period of August 1878 to September 1881 have survived. Continuing the tradition begun when she herself married and left home, Martha carefully saved the letters she and her son received. Likewise, Anna preserved four of her mother's letters and, also, the correspondence Clinton received from his family in Illinois. Although Clinton wrote his family occasionally,

Anna was the more frequent correspondent. Clinton's mother, Nancy Hathaway Stoner, became acquainted with her new daughter-in-law through letters, and confessed to Clinton:

> Don't get jealous of Anna if the most of our letters are directed to her for you know we all love you better than any body and love Anna for your sake and her faithfulness in writing to us and all hope to love her for her own sake when we know her. [27 January 1880]

The extant letters between Martha Wellington and Anna Stoner from 1878 to 1881 reveal growing empathy between mother and daughter. When she left her mother's home to establish a separate household, Anna expressed regret, but tempered it with a promise: "All I hate about going over there is leaving you but there will be a way provided for you to be taken care of Ma as sure as there is a God in heaven" [7 October 1878]. Later, after Martha also left the house that her late husband had built in Refugio County for a new home on the opposite side of the San Antonio River, she received comfort from her daughter's correspondence, and professed to Anna: "It is such a pleasure to me to be able to hear from you often and to get such *cheering* letters that I cannot help being much happier here than I was over on the other side" [6 April 1880]. Continuing the practice followed when Anna was a schoolgirl, Martha used letters to advise her daughter in the ways of womanhood, but more gently than before. Anna reciprocated with precise accounts of successful ways in which she fulfilled her role and even proffered occasional practical advice to her mother.

Anna's letters to Martha were markedly different from Thomas's letters to their mother. Thomas Wellington wrote his mother as he traveled between the Texas towns of Refugio, San Diego, Lockhart, and Austin, selling cattle and horses. His six letters and cards to Martha during 1878–1881 were brief, objective accounts of his trips and work, with occasional references to problems with his health. These letters disclosed little about how he felt about his work or his poor health. After 1881, as diabetes gradually disabled him, Thomas more definitely expressed the emotions he experienced, especially his frustration and despair; but while he continued to work and travel from 1878 to 1881, his letters remained impassive reports.

Writing paper and postage stamps were precious commodities for the Wellingtons and Stoners. Anna's stationery was usually a lined sheet eight inches long and ten inches wide, folded in half to create four writing surfaces. After she filled every line with pen or pencil, Anna completed her letters using all the margins on each page. Then, if she needed to write more, she rotated the page and wrote vertically over the horizontal script. Once, Anna had to use paper in which mice had nibbled holes. The three-cent postage required to mail letters during 1878–1881 was often an extravagance for the Stoners. When possible, Anna saved the cost of buying postage by sending letters to her mother with neighbors traveling in the Wellingtons' direction. Upon completing one letter, Anna discovered she could not afford the necessary postage because Clinton had spent all their extra money for a tooth extraction. When she could afford postage, Anna sent letters with Clinton on his occasional trips into Victoria. When neighboring men and women went into town, they, too, often carried the Stoners' letters to the post office and returned with their mail. At times, days or even weeks passed between the time Anna wrote a letter and the time it was finally sent to the post office. The envelopes originally used for Anna's early correspondence no longer accompany the letters, and the inner address is the only extant evidence of where the Stoners lived during 1878–1881. Rather than naming the nearest post office, Anna used the words *Fair View, Curd Place,* and *At home* to indicate place names familiar to her mother and brother.

Anna's written language and style reflected her reading, which consisted largely of newspapers and periodicals. The

Stoners owned few books during their married years and the length of their work day allowed little time for reading, but both Clinton and Anna found time to enjoy some of the popular press of their era. Nancy H. Stoner sent her son and daughter-in-law subscriptions to the Decatur, Illinois, *Democrat*, wherein Anna read about the social events involving Clinton's family; a beekeeping journal, from which Clinton ordered supplies for his apiary; and *The Household*, from which Anna collected recipes, dress patterns, and health remedies.[2] Anna also avidly read *The Victoria Advocate*, through which she kept up with current events, and another publication entitled *Gleanings*. The influence of the journalistic style of her main reading materials is evident in Anna's letters as she recounts the details of daily events. While her reading often influenced word choices in her letters, Anna's spelling was usually more phonetic than trained. She abbreviated often, using & for *and*, *Vic* for *Victoria*, and initials in place of full names, when she knew her mother would recognize them, in order to save time and precious writing paper. Anna used commas more liberally than periods, which seldom interrupted the flow of her words.

The primary purpose of Anna Stoner's letters as a young bride was to maintain continuity with her mother and brother and the community of her childhood. In addition, however, her letters from 1878 to 1881 serve historians well by answering specific questions concerning the commonplace details of housing and furnishings, foodways, clothing, health care, and family and neighborhood relationships experienced by an ordinary Texas farm family. Everyday activities, dictated by the immediate requirements of livestock and the cyclical pattern of crop production, were often monotonous for rural families. The occasional arrival of visitors brought welcomed breaks in the daily routine. The Stoners moved three times during the first four years of their marriage, each move taking them progressively further into Victoria County and away from Anna's birthplace in Refugio County. As they moved, they accumulated more and more of the household goods and farm tools necessary for their comfort and support. Frequent lack of cash caused postponement of improvements in the family's incommodious housing until the allocation of profits, if any, from their primary cash crop, cotton. Purchases of clothing materials and home furnishings depended upon the availability of extra produce for barter or sale.

In the Stoner household, prevalent nineteenth-century gender roles dictated the division of day-long labor required to provide food for the family table. Like other rural families, they subsisted primarily on grains, vegetables, and fruits they themselves grew and preserved and on chicken, pork, and beef they raised and butchered. Fish, wild birds, and other game often supplemented their diet. After the annual harvest, Clinton Stoner traveled to the town of Victoria to purchase staple goods, such as salt, coffee, flour, and sugar. Also in Victoria, Clinton bought clothing materials for Anna to fashion into appropriate work and social attire. In the well-understood code of nineteenth-century femininity, appearance indicated character, and a vital part of every young woman's education was the art of sewing small, strong stitches. Rural Texas women like Anna learned to improvise with the least expensive materials they could acquire and learned to remake clothing to fit new needs, new styles, new sizes. They deftly refashioned outgrown or outmoded clothing into aprons or children's clothes until the material became so worn that it was thrown into the quilting bag.

Because all members of a rural family contributed something to the work of the farm, their health and strength was of vital importance. Anna's letters indicated the extent to which contagious viruses, unwholesome drinking water, poor diets, and sheer exhaustion threatened the well-being of farm families living in the coastal lowlands. In addition, unpredictable fluctuations of cold and hot weather and occasional storms with high winds endangered families and property along the coast. Dealing with unruly livestock caused frequent injuries among farmers, and infestations of mosquitoes, fleas, weevils, mice, and rats further frustrated residents in the country. Because trained physicians were few and scattered in rural areas, the role of guardian of the family's health fell upon women, who, like Anna, relied on skills and knowledge passed down by their mothers or, in some cases, on experimentation and common sense. The Wellington-Stoner correspondence illustrates ways rural neighbors and relatives aided one another when illness or misfortune struck. Families assumed their ill neighbors' chores in addition to their own work and took turns keeping vigil over the sick or injured throughout the night, giving respite to family caregivers.

Just as neighbor helped neighbor during health crises, they also exchanged labor, produce, and advice. Communication between relatives and neighbors required interruption of a busy family's work, but provided the family with considerable information on subjects ranging from stock prices to local gossip. During the first four years of their marriage, the Stoners had frequent contact with Stoner relatives, with women Anna had known as a schoolgirl, and with families who were her father's former patients. Through constant work, along with some creativity and the help of family and friends, Anna and Clinton together provided their own sustenance and contributed to their neighbors' welfare, while simultaneously adjusting to married life in the midst of cultural change.

Tolerably Comfortable
1877–1878

When Clinton Stoner married Anna Wellington on 28 November 1877, he offered her the life of a farm wife in a region of Texas where farming was difficult at best and, in fact, an unprofitable occupation. For the first ten months of their marriage, the Stoners lived with Anna's mother and brother at the Wellington home in Refugio County. Settlement of Royal Wellington's estate remained incomplete three years after the doctor's death. Finally, in May 1878, the family members, who apparently disputed the division of the estate, signed an agreement allowing their neighbors, Peter Fagan and Dennis O'Connor, to arbitrate their differences. Fagan and O'Connor decreed that Martha Wellington owed Anna and Clinton Stoner the amount of $64.85 and that Thomas Wellington owed his mother $203.70. As soon as the family agreed upon the monies owed, they accepted the distribution of the land and stock. The settlement, signed on 23–24 May 1878, divided Wellington's original 1,004 acres into three strips, each beginning with a narrow frontage on the San Antonio River and rising to a long, rolling prairie. Thomas received 251 acres of land on the lower side of the tract, eleven head of cattle, and two horses. Anna received 251 acres of land on the upper side of the tract, twelve head of cattle, and three horses. Martha kept the middle portion, amounting to 502 acres, and the homestead.[3]

Like many of their neighbors, the Wellingtons and Stoners suffered frequently from infectious viruses and malaria that plagued the Texas lowlands. During the spring of 1878, Martha Wellington contracted an illness that continued into the hot, humid summer months. In July, she journeyed to Aransas Bay for a period of recuperation that lasted until late fall. In the busy coastal village of Lamar, Martha lived at the hotel, operated at that time by the Henry Kroeger family.[4] She took her meals—cornbread, milk, and occasional butter and fresh meat—with other boarders, and soon learned that life in a hotel called for self-reliance and meant close competition at mealtime. She wrote Anna:

> About three weeks ago I got up in the night to close the window when it was raining & in the dark I had a fall which cut a gash in my right brow & bruised my face very much but it is nearly well now—Mrs. [Henrietta] Little

put on some sticking plaster & closed the cut place up as
well as she could & washed it with Castile soap for me—I
went to see her as soon as I got my breakfast as there was
no one here to do any thing for me—I was a perfect sight
to appear at table before so many men (& all strangers) for
a week or two but if I wanted to fare as well as the rest I
had to be at the first table. [11 October 1878]

Meanwhile, in Martha's absence, Anna managed the household
tasks on the Wellington farm, including caring for the chickens,
cooking, sewing, laundering, and gardening. Clinton did what
he knew best, farming, on the strip of land Anna had inherited
from her father's estate. Thomas Wellington alternated clerk-
ing in small stores in the Anaqua vicinity and working for
neighboring ranchers, rounding up their cattle and mustangs
and driving them to various Texas towns for sale.

While living at her mother's home through the summer of
1878, Anna took seriously her responsibility for the care of the
chickens, including those belonging to her mother, but her husband and brother apparently considered the chickens trouble-
some. In the self-sustaining economy of the farm, poultry held
a very important place, and the burden of feeding and protecting them usually fell to the women of the household. Besides
using the flesh and eggs for meals, women used chicken feathers for stuffing pillows and mattresses and sold or bartered
both eggs and pullets. Any accident or illness that threatened
her chickens was a major calamity to Anna Stoner. In one letter to Martha in Lamar, Anna reported three incidents that
endangered their brood. First, she lost seventeen chickens one
night when their roosting box tipped over on top of them—a
suspicious incident, which Anna could not explain. She wrote,
"the mistery is how did the box get turned over there was no
horse staked near there that night & I don't see how it hap-
pened." Then, when Clinton found his mother-in-law's red
rooster in his cornfield eating pumpkins, he threw a bone at
the culprit, hitting it on the head and killing it. Remorsefully,

Clinton brought the dead rooster to Anna in the house, where the young couple agreed that they would give Martha her choice of their two roosters to replace the one killed. Next, Thomas discovered a blue pullet roosting on the stable, hit it with a stick, and broke its leg [5 August 1878]. Only a month later, Anna reported to Martha that the chickens suffered from "the sore head." To treat them, she pulled out their wing feathers and fed them corn, a remedy with successful results [10 September 1878].

By late summer 1878, when they realized that Anna was pregnant with their first child, the Stoners began looking for their own place to live and farm. On Saturday, 17 August 1878, while Thomas was away from the farm on business, Clinton and Anna traveled by wagon to Victoria to purchase things they would need to set up housekeeping. They left word for Thomas that they would return on Sunday, but just after they arrived in the bustling city, Clinton contracted bilious fever. Until Clinton recovered sufficiently to return home the next week, he and Anna found lodging at the home of the Garnett family, longtime friends of the Wellingtons. In the meantime, Thomas returned to an empty house, and when his sister and her husband had not returned by Tuesday, 20 August, he began inquiring about them. No one among their friends in Anaqua or their relatives in Kemper's Bluff knew of their whereabouts, so he kept looking until he found them at the Garnetts' home. Writing his mother on Thursday evening, 22 August, Thomas reported that he had sat up all night with Clinton.[5] Three weeks later, the Stoners returned home but Clinton was still ill. In spite of his weakness, he drove the wagon over to Robert Bello's home in Victoria County to get medicine. Skeptical of physicians, Anna wrote Martha, "I hope if he is any thing of a Dr. that he will give him some thing to cure him."

In addition to news of Clinton's bout with bilious fever, Martha received news from Anna of widespread illness throughout

Refugio and Victoria counties. At the Stoner Pasture Company, Clinton's relatives were all sick, except James Crawford, the husband of Clinton's cousin, Nannie Harris Stoner Crawford. James complained to Anna and Anna reported to Martha that at the ranch headquarters, "they are all sick and all a shouting." At the same time, five of Anna's neighbors were ill and one neighbor was near death [10 September 1878]. Likewise, Thomas wrote Martha a week later that when he visited Mission Refugio in September, he found his friends there suffering chills and heard reports of yellow fever cases in Corpus Christi [17 September 1878]. As the wife of a physician, Martha had received much exposure to illnesses and their remedies, and she believed she had special competence in the ways of health care. In October 1878, an epidemic arose in Lamar, and the local doctor, J. A. Clarke, could not keep up with the caseload. The death of Mrs. Wells, who, Martha wrote Anna, "kept medicines of all kinds and doctored people," left Clarke without assistance. Families with medical emergencies began requesting that Martha, along with the local school teacher, Jane O'Connor, and Martha's friend, Henrietta Little, nurse patients and instruct family caretakers "what was best for the sick." In terms of her own convalescence, Martha believed that Clarke was overcautious, because, as she wrote Anna, "*he* don't know everything" [11 October 1878].

Delayed for a month by Clinton's illness, the Stoners finally moved from Anna's childhood home in late September 1878 to a decrepit house at Fair View, the Cromwell's farm near Anaqua. There they both shared responsibilities harvesting crops belonging to Clinton's relatives. Anna drove a wagon up and down between two rows of corn, keeping a little bit ahead or even with Clinton, who followed on foot, pulling ears from both rows and piling them in the wagon bed. Together they picked peas, also, until an asp, "as poisonous as a snake," stung Clinton's neck. When the venom spread, Anna had to find help to carry Clinton into the house. After one long day's work in

the fields, Anna sat down and wrote her mother a letter carefully describing her first home as an independent, married
woman. Although she had to pen her letter around holes
chewed in her paper by mice, Anna boasted to her mother
about Clinton's efforts to make the house livable, in the following way:

> I am housekeeping now up in this little house. Clinton has
> fixed it up as well as he could & it does very well, he dug
> the dirt out from under it, & raised the lower part & put
> new sleepers and sills under it & took out the bottom
> blocks & put rock under it; the floor is as level as it ever
> was he took away the board window & put a sash there in
> the end, you know . . . he has boarded up the place where
> the chimney was & torn the old chimney away. Clint fixed
> all the cracks that he could, so you see it is tolerable com-
> fortable for this kind of wether.

The single mention of the house's furnishings in Anna's letter
to Martha was her comment on the stove: "My stove does fine
we were very careful about heating it at first, it is the same
number as yours (No. 7) but it seems to be larger & all the
cooking vessels are bigger" [7 October 1878].

As she wrote on 7 October 1878 about her house at Fair
View, Anna already knew that her stay there was temporary.
As soon as they completed the harvest, the Stoners moved to
one hundred acres of Victoria County prairie land, which
Clinton rented for twelve dollars per year from physician John
Curd, who moved his family into town. Clinton took Anna to
see the Curd house before he agreed to rent it. Compared to
Fair View, Anna found the new place, a former dog-trot cabin,
to be a step up in comfort: "[The Curd place] has two rooms &
a hall between all sealed & a back galery full length of the
house with a little room out of the end west, the kitchen is
joined to the house by a little galery that is roofed over" [7

October 1878]. At Fair View, Anna and Clinton had carried drinking water from a neighbor's well and other water from a nearby spring; but at the Curd place, they collected water from a bucket lowered by pulley into a roofed cistern situated next to the porch connecting the house and the kitchen. A fence separated the house from the fields.

At the Curd place, Clinton and Anna Stoner spent their first Christmas in their own household. The weather was cold, and Anna, being pregnant, was unwilling to risk becoming chilled on the drive to the Stoner family's celebration at James and Nancy Crawford's home in the Stoner Pasture Company compound. Anna declined other invitations to holiday gatherings as well. On the Sunday before Christmas, she and Clinton received visitors, including the Miller family from near Anaqua. "All went 'as merry as a marriage bell,'" Anna wrote her mother, "except Mrs. M. went off with a high head, clouded brow & sharp words because I would not promise to go to her big Xmas dinner, so so, 'every cloud has a silver lineing.'" After the holidays passed and the weather warmed for a few days, Anna visited the Crawfords to hear about the festivities she had missed. She saw the remnants of a ceiling-high Christmas tree that had been decorated with transparent flags and varicolored candles. Anna assured her mother, however, that she and Clinton enjoyed their own private holiday celebration. On the Monday before Christmas Day, Clinton brought from town a barrel of flour, fifty pounds of sugar, and a keg of molasses. Anna spent the cold days of Christmas week before her cozy wood stove, baking cakes [7 January 1879].

Independent of Them All
1879

Anna and Clinton entered the year 1879 with a sense of well-being and expectation. Just after the first of January, they received from Clinton's family in Illinois a much-welcomed gift box. Anna invited Martha to "come over soon & see what all *was* in it," adding, "it surprised me *very pleasantly* I can assure you." Anna boasted, "I've got bed clothing by the wholesale an[d] the new bedstead is *new* all over and the old one shines under its new quilt. We are fixed for company now" [7 January 1879].

A ten-month lapse exists in the extant correspondence of Anna and her mother from January to November 1879. For many of those months, Martha Wellington apparently stayed with Anna, helping her daughter during her confinement before, during, and after the birth of her first child, a daughter, born on 22 April 1879. Following the practice of many nineteenth-century families, the Stoners waited to record formally the name of their infant until she was several months old. In November 1879, when the baby was seven months old, Anna directed her mother to add her name to the family Bible as Hope Augusta [27 November 1879]. Anna chose her daughter's name in honor of her cousin, Augusta Betts, whom she had visited in Hope, Arkansas.

No written evidence exists of Anna's pregnancy, confinement, or childbirth experience. B. T. Davis or Robert Bello, physicians often mentioned in Anna's letters, may have assisted the birth of Anna's baby, or perhaps Martha Wellington served as midwife for her grandchild's birth. Although Anna's letters do not contain her feelings about her own safety in childbirth, they do mention frequent miscarriages and deaths during childbirth that occurred among Anna's female friends and Clinton's female relatives. Having borne eight children, only six of whom lived past childhood, Nancy H. Stoner understood the seriousness of childbirth for women in her day, and upon hearing of her grandchild's successful birth, expressed her relief to Anna and Clinton as follows:

> It is strange Anna you had not received my letter before you wrote to me. I answered yours and Clintons letters

you wrote before you were sick, and the letter he wrote on
or after the birth of little Hope was not answered, my
anxiety was so great for Anne. When I read your letter
my son and found all was *over* and all doing well and so
hopefull my strength went forth in one *great Amen* and
thankfulness to him who is ever mercifull and I was weak
as a little child, not fit for anything for two or three days.

Furthermore, Nancy Stoner offered her son the following specific instruction in parenting, revealing at the same time her
own personal attitude toward gender relationships:

My son if you want your little Hope to say Mother always
call Anna Mother in her presence. If you want her to be a
lover of musick, sing sweet songs to her in her infancy and
if you wish her to be all that is good and pure teach it to
her by example, and when she grows older teach her not
to fear man, as a great many mothers do, but teach her to
make men fear her. [25 May 1879]

For her part, Nancy Stoner, who always referred to Clinton's
father as "Mr. Stoner," complained in letters to her children of
her husband's frequent absences from home on fishing and
hunting trips and of his inattention to her physical ailments,
which she attributed to her "change of life." Envisioning a different way of life for her granddaughter, Nancy hoped that
Clinton would assume responsibility to teach his daughter to
become a woman towards whom men would demonstrate the
kind of respect that generations of women before her had
shown to the fathers, brothers, and sons in their lives.

In spite of the absence of letters during most of 1879, an indication of the Stoners' and Wellingtons' activities exists in
court records. On 20 March 1879, a month before Hope's birth,
Anna and Clinton sold Anna's inherited land on the San Antonio River to William Avery for $340.32 cash and a promissory
note for $434.68 due with interest of 10 percent per annum on

or before 15 November 1879. On 28 April 1879 Thomas Wellington sold the lower portion of his father's estate. Then, on 18 June 1879, the Stoners registered the livestock brand, $\overline{\wedge}$, in Victoria County, in Anna's name. The E-T-A-L brand, signifying the initials of the names Elizabeth, Thomas, and Anna Louisa, remained Anna's brand throughout her life.[6]

No deed record exists indicating that the Stoners subsequently purchased land with the profits made from the sale of their Refugio County land. The cash proceeds were probably insufficient for the purchase of a farm of equal size in more prosperous Victoria County, so Anna and Clinton applied part of the money to the lease of a farm and part to improvements in the house and increases in their livestock. Their new location was to remain their home for two and a half years. Although Anna used only the words *At home* in her letters from Victoria County, rather than naming the nearest post office, information from her correspondence compared with other public and published evidence indicates that the farm's location was in a rural neighborhood on the east side of the Guadalupe River as it flowed in a southeasterly direction toward San Antonio Bay. In their new home, Anna and Clinton lived within sight and sound of other farms. Writing at her kitchen table, Anna described for her mother a typical evening in her neighborhood: "I am writing by lamp light now & Clinton is out feeding the hogs it is dim twilight out of doors but with the hogs squeeling him whistling & all the chickens at a half dozen houses crowing it sounds like bright daylight" [14 September 1880].

Anna's letters indicated that her closest neighbors included the families of Volney Jefferson Rose, Levin and Dora Fromme, James L. and Mollie Gartrell, Joe and Nannie Jordan, and John and Alabama Hunt. Others nearby with whom the Stoners had close contact were Hiram Austin, W. G. Venable, and B. T. Davis. Data from the 1880 census and contemporary writings located these families along the eastern side of the Guadalupe River about midway between the town of Victoria to the north and the Calhoun County line on the south.[7] The Stoners had several family connections in their new neighborhood, one of whom may have been their lessor. Their closest neighbor, Volney J. Rose, was the brother of Zilpa Rose Stoner, the wife of Clinton's cousin, George Overton Stoner. Likewise, Volney was the brother of Lillie Blanche Rose Cromwell, the wife of the Wellingtons' neighbor Francis Hawkins Cromwell. Volney's wife, Mary Lulu Kay Rose, was the daughter of Anne Elizabeth Hunt Kay Stoner, Clinton's "Aunt Lizzie," the second wife of Michael Lowery Stoner. Prior to Anna and Clinton's move to the neighborhood, Mary Rose died, leaving Volney the single parent of three daughters and a son.[8] Lizzie Stoner, her sons Hunt and Davis Stoner, and her brother, John Hunt, and his family lived close enough to exchange frequent visits with Anna and Clinton. Furthermore, the wife of James L. Gartrell was Mollie Payne, the daughter of George Ann Stoner Payne, who was the sister of Nancy Michael Stoner Cromwell of Anaqua, Clinton's father's cousin, with whom he stayed when he first moved to Texas. Only the Frommes' farm separated Anna and Clinton's home from that of the Gartrells.[9]

In November 1879, William Avery paid the balance due the Stoners on the sale of their land in Refugio County, and in December, Clinton began adding improvements to their house. Clinton tore away an old log house on the property and hired Irish carpenter Thomas Boyle to add a stable and wagon shed to the corncrib and build shelves in the front room and bedroom of the house. A welcomed addition to their furnishings came in late November with the arrival of a Stuart Singer sewing machine with attachments, given to Anna by her mother. Having sold the center half of the Wellington farm to rancher Thomas O'Connor on 19 November, Martha used a portion of her profits to purchase the machine for Anna and one just like it for herself.[10] Martha considered the sewing machine's greatest value to be as a symbol of freedom from the necessity of borrowing the machines of certain other women, and therefore becoming indebted to them, an idea she revealed to Anna as follows:

> Mrs. T[ruman] P[helps] wanted to know why you did not go to see her. She said you ought to have taken your sewing up there and just rattled off 'on her machine'—But we will soon be independent of all of them—I hope, you hope and *baby* Hope, don't you? [25 November 1879]

Anna placed the new machine in her dining room and first used it to patch worn clothing and then to create box-pleated window curtains. She had mixed feelings about the expense of the machine, which cost forty-five dollars. After thanking her mother, Anna wrote: "Well Ma you know how I am I am rejoiced & I am sad. I rejoiced to get a machine & to have you give it to me makes it a thousand fold dearer, but it makes me sad to think it is that much taken from you" [27 November 1879]. With the machine, Martha sent Anna a bundle of yard goods for making baby clothes, including "blue opera flowered for a dress and sacque and yellow to line a calico cloak with sleeves and hood." Along with the material came some motherly advice: "[It would be better to] deny yourself the pleasures of the anticipated Hollowdays (as I used to do for you) than to run any *risk* to her *health*. Then you will have a *clear conscience* & be much *happier* for it" [25 November 1879]. In her answering letter, written while Clinton was away hunting duck on a nearby bayou, Anna assured her mother that "Christmas or not," she would take care of Hope. In fact, she refused to "*run any risk whatever* with her," and therefore, would decline an invitation for Christmas dinner at George and Zilpa Stoner's ranch home. To prove her point further, she enumerated the long-sleeved, high-necked flannel shirts and the flannel underskirts she had sewn to keep the baby warm throughout the coming winter. Also, Anna knitted woolen stockings and promised her mother she would keep them on Hope until the return of warm weather [27 November 1879].

When Hope suffered occasional chills and fever, Anna treated her successfully with patent medicines and tonics, including paregoric and magnesia. She herself complained only of infrequent colds or neuralgia. Clinton, however, became ill more often and more seriously than his wife and daughter, and Anna usually sent for the doctor to treat him, believing that most of his illnesses resulted from poor judgment or overwork. Before daybreak on the Sunday morning before Thanksgiving 1879, Clinton awoke with severe intestinal cramps. Unable to ease his pain with her own remedies, Anna ran through the dark to the Frommes' home and asked Levin to go for the doctor. Leaving her own seven children alone, Dora Fromme accompanied Anna home across the fields to help with Clinton, whose suffering was great. The two women applied all their known remedies to relieve him, including forcing him to inhale camphor and drink hot toddies, piling hot ashes on the pit of his stomach, and bathing his feet in hot water. Anna later confessed to her mother that she had feared that Clinton would die before the doctor arrived. Finally, after daybreak, Fromme and Davis came, and the doctor gave Clinton medicine that relieved his pain quickly. Upon questioning Clinton, Davis discovered that the cause of his colic and distress was not an infection, but had resulted from Clinton's having eaten "a stalk of frosted sugar cane" [27 November 1879].

By the end of 1879, the Stoners had become contributing participants in the life of their rural neighborhood. Just as the Frommes had aided the Stoners during Clinton's bout with indigestion from eating spoiled sugar cane, both Anna and Clinton sat up through the night attending sick neighbors. Just two weeks after his own illness and while he still suffered from dysentery, Clinton sat up through the night with young Willie Hunt, who was injured by his horse while trying to pen a milk calf [14 December 1879]. Anna, too, sat up with the ill children of neighboring women, allowing the weary mothers time to rest.

In addition to sharing aid when sickness struck neighbors, rural women exchanged homemaking ideas. From Dora Fromme, Anna received a recipe for light bread made with cornmeal, which Anna then passed on to her mother in her Thanksgiving letter. The recipe combined six teacups of cornmeal and five cups of warm water, leavened with half a cup of cornmeal sourdough. Anna placed the dough in a pan on a shelf behind the wood stove to rise. When it had risen, she sifted ten cups of flour and worked it into the dough, along with a sprinkle of salt. Then, Anna allowed the bread to bake slowly in the oven, which was heated just enough to keep the dough rising [27 November 1879].

Families in the Stoners' neighborhood further cooperated by trading seeds and excess produce from family gardens and orchards, sharing remedies for curing livestock ailments, helping locate stray livestock, and dividing butchering chores. Writing to her mother on Thanksgiving Day 1879, Anna reported that Clinton had sold to their neighbors for two dollars apiece several turkeys she had raised. Besides turkeys, the Stoners added hogs to their livestock, and hog raising and butchering became a cooperative effort between the Stoners and their neighbors. The first hard freeze of winter signaled hog-killing time. In December 1879, Anna and Clinton shared tasks with their German-American neighbors, the Frommes, to kill and render five hogs, an endeavor Anna cleverly labeled "Stoner and Fromme," as though the two couples had formed a joint business enterprise. Another neighbor, Solomon Gant, also helped with the butchering. The results, Anna wrote Martha, were "lots of fresh *hog* from top end to hoof tip with sausages, cracklins and meat lard [and] skins for soap juice." Hog butchering was a familiar annual task for Clinton, whose family raised hogs on their farm in Macon County, Illinois. However, hog-killing was a new experience for Anna, so she wrote her mother a detailed account of the process and her role in it, as follows:

> Clinton cut it all up while I cut up the beef fat & he skined all of the other meat fat for lard as he picked it out from the sausage meat he skined it by haveing a sharpe case knife & taken a strip half as wide as this paper [about three inches] lay the skin part flat on the table & after starting it enough to take a good hold just worked the meat from side to side holding to the skin alone & holding knife perfectly still with the left hand & haveing it lay flat on the table. Clinton ground up all of the sausage meat himself & as he was finishing Mr. Gant came along & as soon as I seasoned it they stuffed it & fixed it to hang up. We are going to smoke our meat at Mr. F[romme]'s. [14 December 1879]

With help from their neighbors, the Stoners approached the end of 1879 with a full larder. For the second year in a row, Christmas brought weather too cold for Anna to visit her mother and brother or Clinton's relatives. After Christmas, a brief warm spell allowed time for Clinton and neighboring men, Jordan, Venable, Gartrell, and Fromme, to build a bridge across a nearby bayou to an island where they planned to keep their hogs. When the next year's hog season arrived, Clinton would choose five or six hogs from the island herd to fatten in a pen near the house.

A Little House Well Filled
1880

In January 1880, Anna hoped to spend her birthday, Saturday, the seventeenth, visiting her mother and brother, but a sudden winter rain flooded the river, preventing Anna from making the trip. On days when winter weather confined her to the house, Anna spent long hours sewing for Hope. Now nine months old, Hope had cut two baby teeth, could almost stand up, and was fat and playful, as Anna illustrated for Martha with the following anecdote:

> Yesterday after dinner I sat the baby on the table with her back to the wall & moved every thing out of the way so she couldn't reach any thing & then went in the kitchen about 15 minutes after I looked in there to see what she was doing I thought she was very quiet & there she had drawn a saucer of stewed pumpkin up to her & the most of it out on the table & in her lap had both hand & mouth full & was licking in the other just as fast as she could. I didn't say a word to her & took a dirty cup towel & began to wipe her off & then such fighting as she did try to do & how she did grab at it. I took it away & now [illegible] . . . she will spit out pumpkin at the table nearly all the time, it is the first time she ever got in mischief. [n.d. January 1880]

The long winter nights afforded Clinton the first opportunity in six months to write his mother. Nancy Stoner responded promptly to her son's letter and, as usual, offered him some advice, this time concerning ways to spend Sundays rather than working. If he wanted something to do, she suggested, "Take your wife who needs recreation & go to church and if you are deprived of that get some good reading from bible, the Household or Brick and seat your selves in your own little home and make each other happy." Furthermore, she exhorted, "after your dinner is over *walk down to Mrs. Morrows* or to *mothers* or *write* your own dear mother who is ever longing to hear from *you* and *yours*" [n.d. 1880].

During January 1880, Anna and Clinton learned the importance of timing in marketing their livestock, and the occasion inspired Anna to share what she had learned with her brother,

Thomas. That month the Stoners sold neighboring rancher Hiram Austin their two-year-old cattle for ten dollars each and their four-year-old cattle for sixteen dollars apiece. Austin told Clinton that if he had sold his stock two months earlier, the price would have been higher. In November the younger ones would have sold for sixteen dollars each, and the older ones for twenty. In the single extant letter from Anna to her brother during her years in Victoria County, she advised Thomas, based on Clinton's experience, to invest in cattle rather than land, warning him to "always do a little calculating before you act and keep your eyes open." She suggested that Thomas and Martha, both of whom were looking for ways to use the money earned from the sales of their portions of the Wellington estate, buy cows with calves at the current market price of ten or eleven dollars and sell the calves for veal for five or six dollars each. Rather than buy land for their herd, Anna encouraged her family to rent pasture from her neighbor, Joe Jordan, who would let them use his land for less than a dollar a year or eight cents a month. Renting in her neighborhood had the advantage for stock raising, Anna wrote, because it was "here close to the rail rode where they will be more in demand" [21 January 1880].[11]

Although Thomas was the older of the two Wellington children, he lacked Anna's ambitious, optimistic spirit. His younger sister employed her letter to encourage Thomas to act promptly and positively in order to gain the best financial advantage for his investments. Anna then extended her sisterly advice with an appeal that summarized the pragmatic philosophy which she had formulated since her marriage:

> Learn to think for yourself Brother & dont *tell* everything
> you intend doing, for if you do some one will do it for you
> if there is any money in it & if there is'nt they will say 'let
> him do it if he wants to it will teach him some sence.' . . .
> dont sit still & wait for some one to offer to sell you their

stock but go find out what they will sell for & if it is to much make them fall if you can. Be up & stiring you know what the past has been & what the present is *now make the future something better.*

Leaving the past behind and adjusting to changes in the present became a way of life for Anna and Thomas's mother after the death of their father. After she sold her portion of the old Wellington farm in November 1879, Martha Wellington had written Anna, "I am anxious to get away from this place and all the disagreeable associations connected with it for they will never end as long as I stay" [25 November 1879]. In a later letter to Anna, Martha reiterated her discontent, stating, "Do not *imagine for a moment* that I regretted leaving the *old place.* I never left any place with a lighter heart." The reason for her strong negative feelings toward her former home lay in changes among her neighbors, and she explained, "I knew we could not live in peace living between two such families as B. A. on one side and Thor'T. C. on the other as Mr. E. T. M. rented to *Thornton*" [6 April 1880]. Martha did not explain why she disliked the families living on either side of her, probably because she knew Anna would know the reason by the reputation of the names. Martha waited to move until the next spring. Not willing to abandon completely her home of twenty-five years, she dug up some honeysuckle vines and rose bushes from her garden and carried them with her across the San Antonio River to Victoria County. There she and Thomas lived in a small house on twenty acres near their longtime friends, David F. and Amanda Kemper Williams. Because her mother's small house was less comfortable than her former one, Anna sought to make Martha feel better about its size by writing: "Don't worry about your little house. Don't you remember what Burns said about 'a little house well filled.' "[12] Anna went on to describe for her mother how filled her own four-room home had become. Even though her front room now held sacks

69

of cotton seed and seed corn as well as beehives and beekeeping implements, Anna considered it "very respectable looking." Her dining room and kitchen contained more beekeeping boxes and frames, and under the bed in her bedroom, secure from mice, were dozens of pumpkins. Anna added that the Jordans' home was even more crowded than her own because Joe, the miller, stored cog wheels and milling implements in the kitchen. Such inconveniences were bearable, Anna wrote, because they were only temporary: "Let them put their things away now and maby they can get a place to put them sometime" [27 March 1880].

In her reply to Anna, Martha stated that she would not grumble about "a little house well-filled" as long as they had "a little field well tilled." In addition to the twenty acres surrounding her home, Martha rented ten fenced acres from David Williams. With the help of their regularly hired worker, Irish-born John D. Brady, and a temporarily recruited Mexican-American laborer, Austacio Martinez, Thomas plowed his mother's fields, which, she complained, were infested with fleas and overgrown with weeds. The soil in the hogwallow was so hard that Martha's hens could not scratch there, and she had to feed them a supplement of bran and toasted egg shells to promote laying. "Want of water," Martha wrote Anna, "is our greatest trouble." Their new location had neither well nor cistern. For drinking, Thomas or his helpers brought Martha "a little blue keg full from the river every day"; for cooking, they hauled water to the house from Francisco Ticerino's well; and for washing, they used water from a nearby lake [6 April 1880].

In contrast to her mother's situation, Anna felt that she and her husband possessed both a well-filled home and a well-tilled field. Clinton was relaxed, no longer prone to worrying "like he used to" and "happier now than he ever has been in Tex[as]." Anna claimed credit for her husband's sense of well-being, which she believed resided in his relationship to his wife and daughter, for "when he comes in troubled," she wrote, "he tells me about it and then gets to playing with baby Hope and in a measure forgets it" [20 March 1880]. Hope was a healthy child and Anna was pregnant again and becoming increasingly confident in her abilities as wife and mother. She had so improved her homemaking skills that she could boast, "I flatter myself that I am a better housekeeper now than when we lived at the C[urd] place." Anna summarized her feelings of fulfillment by writing Martha, "Providence has smiled on us in everything" [12 April 1880].

Among the most arduous of Anna's domestic responsibilities was laundering. Like generations of women before her, Anna filled two wash pots with water, built a fire, and boiled the clothes, using lye soap she herself had made. After the clothes dried on the fence or on bushes, Anna ironed them with sadirons heated on her wood stove. She steadied a board between the horizontal slats of the backs of two chairs to create an ironing surface. The weekly washing and ironing was a two-day chore.[13] When rural Texas women could afford to hire domestic help, laundering was the first chore they delegated to others. Martha Wellington, accustomed before the Civil War to assigning laundry chores to slave women, hired Betsy, a former slave, to do her washing. Also, during 1880, nineteen-year-old Helen McNickol earned room and board in the Wellington household by helping Martha with the housework. In exchange for cooking, ironing, cleaning, and milking, Helen received tutoring from Martha when school was not in session. In 1881, a girl named Sallie lived with Martha to help her with her housework. Even with the help of other women, Martha was not completely free of household or farm chores. At the age of fifty-five, she did her own churning and sewing and kept the garden and chickens.

Domestic life was not all drudgery for women like Anna and her mother, but provided occasional outlets for creativity. With characteristic energy, Anna found practical solutions to problems presented by her small home and its sparse furnishings. While she wrote Martha before noon on 12 April 1880, Anna also fixed dinner for Clinton and watched young Hope, who was just beginning to toddle about the house. When Anna momentarily diverted her eyes from Hope, the baby crawled into the fireplace after a kitten and covered her body and clothes with ashes. Anna had to stop writing in order to clean the child and the hearth. In her next letter, Anna explained fully to Martha her solution to the open fireplace. Using materials at hand, she made a frame and covered it with cloth, in the center of which she pasted a picture titled "A Summer Holiday Starting the Team," and then she bordered the scene with brown paper. The picture, probably clipped from a magazine or book, depicted a young couple driving a wagon between a forest and a stream. Four children rode with them in the wagon and two others were in a boat being pulled through the water by ropes attached to the wagon [13 May 1880].

In addition to housekeeping, Anna's areas of responsibility on the farm included feeding chickens, maintaining the garden, and milking the cows. Throughout the year, Anna kept her mother updated on the progress of her gardening. The yearly cycle for the family garden began in the dark days of winter when Anna began ordering seed from the D. M. Ferry Company catalog. In January 1880, she planted mustard, radish, lettuce, cabbage, and parsley seeds in the garden plot Clinton had prepared. She planted tomato and flower seeds in boxes to keep in the house until the ground warmed in the spring. In February, Anna added turnips, beets, English peas, shallots, leeks, beans, okra, and Irish potatoes to her garden. In March, a late freeze destroyed Anna's cucumbers, butter beans, and okra, along with the figs, plums, and peaches in the orchard, but she had saved a supply of seeds for just such an emergency and replanted the lost crops. By April 1880, Anna's garden was in full bloom. Along with her letters that month, Anna sent her mother seeds for pole beans, parsley, ice cream watermelon, nutmeg, musk melon, and beets. In May, Anna sent her mother produce from her garden, including butter beans, beets, and squash. In June, the summer heat dried up the vegetables, and Anna let chickens loose in the garden to forage among the dead plants, signifying the end of the spring garden cycle. The fall garden would consist of pumpkins and potatoes.[14] Year round, Anna's daily chores included milking and churning. When they had excess butter, Clinton sold or bartered it among neighbors and in Victoria.

Maintaining livestock and raising crops occupied most of Clinton's time on the farm. Besides poultry, dairy cows, and hogs, the livestock on the Stoner farm included a team of horses, two mares, and beef cattle. In addition, Clinton managed an impressive thirty-two swarms of bees during 1880. When their stock increased by five newborn calves early in the year, the Stoners once again hired Thomas Boyle, who repaired the field fence and improved the dairy lot. Clinton plowed the fields in February and planted corn and cotton in March. When the spring freeze that had ruined Anna's garden killed his first cotton crop, he, too, replowed and replanted. Corn production was primarily an individual effort on Clinton's part, which Anna chronicled in letters throughout the growing season. In April he swept the corn, in May he laid it by, and in August he pulled and cribbed it. Each day during the harvest of 1880, Anna bragged, Clinton hauled eight wagonloads of corn, with about twelve bushels per load. Throughout the year, Clinton took the dried corn to Jordan's mill for grinding into cornmeal for Anna to use in preparing the family's meals.

Cotton production required outside help. After completing the corn harvest in 1880, Clinton hired Adam and Mary Dean, a couple of African descent, to help him pick the year's cotton crop. The Deans, who rented land from the Stoners for the coming year, moved their house to a plot near the Stoners' pasture gate. The couple had once worked for the Volney Rose family, and, more recently, had labored for John Hunt. Anna

73

wrote her mother that Hunt and Mary "fell out," and the Deans were told to leave the Hunt farm. Although Clinton relied upon the Deans to help harvest his cotton, Anna probably had little to do with Mary. Basing her judgment of the couple on gossip, Anna wrote her mother, "Everyone says he is an excellent negrow but that his wife is too independent to live" [14 September 1880].

Daily responsibilities on their farm kept both Clinton and Anna close to home most of the time, but they managed to maintain fairly close contact with other farmers, neighbors, and relatives. Once the harvest was gathered, Clinton traveled to the mill or the gin with his produce and then to town with his profits, and there he met and mingled with other farmers doing the same thing. With careful planning, Anna found occasional opportunities to exchange gossip and ideas with female friends. When the weather was good, Anna and neighboring women hurried through their morning chores, and after cleaning up the dinner dishes and setting aside their work clothes, donned clean calicos and trimmed hats, dressed the children in their best clothes, and spent an hour or so visiting one another. Emancipation of the slaves, whose labor formerly freed Anna's mother's generation from heavy chores, curtailed the tradition of visiting among Texas women who could not afford to hire help. Anna, understanding that her mother could not visit her friends as often as in antebellum days, wrote, "as Mrs. V[enable] said 'we all know how the ladies have to stay at home now, it is'nt as it used to be' " [20 March 1880]. When time allowed, however, Anna exchanged visits with several of Clinton's aunts and female cousins, most whom she had known since childhood, and with other women in her rural neighborhood.[15]

Occasionally on weekends the Stoners set aside their normal routine and hosted or visited groups of Clinton's relatives. In June 1880, Anna reported to Martha that she had fixed dinner for their kin, including George L. and Tallitha Stoner Whitney and five of their children, Nancy H. Stoner Crawford and her son Michael, and Davis Stoner. Also that month, Anna and Clinton spent a Sunday morning at Lizzie Stoner's home with Lizzie's family connections, Alabama and Ida Hunt, Mattie Smith, and Volney Rose. Following dinner, the younger members of the group moved from Lizzie's home to Alabama's home, where Ida, a seventeen-year-old schoolgirl, played the piano for their entertainment. Anna and Clinton loaded their wagon with extra chairs for the trip from Lizzie's to the Hunts', and when they returned the chairs to Lizzie's, she prepared them a cold supper so large, Anna reported, that Lizzie would have leftovers for days following [25 June 1880].

For visiting friends and receiving guests, Anna clothed herself and her daughter as respectably as her resources allowed. She considered the labor involved in earning the money to buy the material, in creating the clothes by hand or on a treadle machine, and in keeping them clean and repaired all part of the duty required to meet the standards of her rural society. While in Victoria County, Anna used the wagon to make her visits when Clinton could spare it from his work, or rode the sorrel mare her father had given her before his death. Throughout her life, when riding horseback, Anna used a sidesaddle and wore long riding skirts.[16] Ready-made garments were too expensive for the Stoners to buy, but handed-down apparel for Hope and occasional gifts for Anna helped keep them in fashion. Bundles of clothing, needlework, and yard goods arrived a few times a year from Clinton's mother and sisters in Illinois. Nancy Hathaway Stoner also laid aside the outgrown clothes of Clinton's youngest sister, Mattie, who was only four years older than Hope, to send to her granddaughter in Texas. In addition, the daughters of George Overton Stoner passed down their outgrown clothes to Hope. The oldest, Margaret Malinda, or "Maggie," visited Anna and Clinton often and gave Hope a knit sacque for her first Christmas and later sent her a special "ready-made linen lawn dress" [n.d. January and 4 June 1880].

Anna valued having at least one dressy outfit for social occasions. When the March 1880 frost killed most of their crops and the outlook for an adequate income for the year looked momentarily bleak, Anna requested a loan of ten dollars from her mother to buy a hat, shoes, and material for a dress, promising to repay the debt after harvest in the fall. Fortunately for Anna, the money arrived as a gift rather than a loan because a debtor had settled an outstanding account with the Wellington estate, one-fourth of which belonged to Anna. Along with the money, Martha sent her daughter a message encouraging her to emulate the dress of other women of her status in her neighborhood, quoting the familiar rationale, "when in Rome, we must do as the Romans do" [6 April 1880]. Three months passed before Clinton's next trip to Victoria, so summer arrived by the time Anna finally received her cloth and pair of shoes. In the meantime, Martha Wellington sent her daughter dress material and trimmings to "make up prettily" to wear to a community barbecue which was planned in Kemper's Bluff for July 2. Ferriage across the Guadalupe would be free that day, according to Martha, and she invited Anna and Hope to visit her and all of Anna's old friends while they were across the river [5 June 1880]. In her answering letter, Anna told her mother that she would not be attending the barbecue. Hope had been suffering chills and fever while she was cutting several baby teeth at once. Although Anna had given the baby iron tonic, she remained "very weak & fretful." Anna felt that she would get to visit Martha eventually when Hope felt better, because Nancy Crawford had offered to take Anna from the Stoner Pasture Company to Martha's any time she wanted to visit [25 June 1880].

Accepting Nancy's offer, Anna and Hope finally visited Martha in July 1880. By the time they returned home, Anna could report to her mother that "baby Hope is as sasey playful as a cricket haveing got entirely well with her 11 teeth." Some time had passed between the day of Anna's return home and the day she finally wrote Martha, a delay caused by lack of money for postage, which she explained in the following manner:

> I recon you wonder why I havent writen to you before now and think some of us are sick, well I cant give any very good reason for it. I wrote a short letter to Clintons mother two weeks ago & if you believe me that letter is not in the office yet. When Clinton went to town when he went to get his extraction & after he had paid it out of the office he found he had no money to buy postage stamps with so back it had to come but now I immagine I can see them [the stamps] in the distance now, as Overton gave him a check for 10 dollars yesterday.

Also in her letter to Martha, Anna recalled her return trip from southwestern Victoria County. From Martha's home, Anna and Hope, along with a young boy who carried their things, rode to the Crawford's home in the Stoner Pasture Company compound near Kemper's Bluff. Arriving there about noon, Anna paid the boy the fifty cent tip furnished by Martha and sent him back home. Finding James Crawford eating dinner alone in the house, Anna teased him, asking "if he was keeping house," to which he replied, "no the house was keeping itself." His wife Nancy had slipped away to visit her sister, Lillie Stoner Hunt, who lived nearby. "Mr. C got up and stired around to get me some dinner out of the safe," Anna recounted, "but when I told him I could get it he eased off a little & let me eat to suit myself while obligingly ans[wering] all of my questions & asked some himself." After dinner, James took a nap, while Anna waited for Nancy. Upon Nancy's return at two o'clock in the afternoon, Anna received a friendly scolding for not arriving sooner in the day, but, to Martha she confided, "I didn't care though." Anna and Hope spent the night with the Crawfords, and Clinton arrived early the next morning to take them home. To Anna's delight, her young husband declared that her absence had convinced him "he wouldn't be a widower five weeks for nothing on earth." Claiming "he thought that week never would end," Clinton confessed "he can't get along without a wife now." Before Anna and Clinton crossed the Guadalupe to go home, the Crawfords hosted a large family dinner. In attendance, besides Anna, Clinton, Hope, and the Crawfords and their sons, Michael and Wilkerson, were George Overton and Zilpa Stoner and their five children, and Wilkins and Lillie Stoner Hunt and their sons, John and Wilkins. In the evening, they were joined by another of Clinton's cousins, Maria Stoner Lynn, and her daughter Laura, who were on their way to Sunday School with the children of Maria's sister-in-law, Mattie Jones. When Anna, Hope, and Clinton finally went home, they took with them George Overton's eleven-year-old daughter, Maggie, whom Anna reported to Martha was "the easiest child to please" in terms of meals. Anna had worried at first about having enough food in the house for an extra mouth, but she discovered that Maggie's tastes were simple. "All she wanted," Anna wrote Martha, "was cornbread & butter & boil milk & that was about all she got too" [5 August 1880].

With August came the Stoners' busiest time of year. Like his neighbors, Clinton began gathering corn and making plans to pick cotton. In the midst of the harvest, the late summer heat grew oppressive and typhoid fever plagued the countryside. Clinton, Anna wrote Martha, suffered a chill and fever, but he refused to stop pulling and hauling corn; to do so would mean certain financial ruin. Relying on her instincts, Anna "poured peach tree leaf tea down him," finding it "shurer than calomel and quinine." Although he vomited all one day, Anna forced Clinton to drink peach tea and water, claiming the bitter tea made the chills "glad to leave." A few days later, when Clinton saw B. T. Davis drive up to the Frommes' house to attend one of their sick children, he walked over to ask the doctor what he should do about his own continuing illness. Davis told Clinton to keep out of the sun for a full day, take quinine, and continue drinking Anna's peach tea, because it was "as good a thing as he could take" [6 September 1880].

The Stoners warded off the effects of typhoid, but their neighbors were not so fortunate. Sickness prevailed in the Fromme and Gartrell households throughout the summer of 1880, and in September, typhoid claimed the life of Eddie Jordan, the miller's six-year-old son. During Eddie's illness, Jordan closed his grist mill, and for a brief time the Stoners hired a boy to go into town for their cornmeal. Anna reported to her mother that B. T. Davis stayed with Eddie three long nights, trying to break the fever, but the child died at three o'clock the third night in a congestive chill. Anna joined other neighbor women, including Davis's wife, in visiting the child and his family during his illness, but the Stoners were the only family in the neighborhood not represented at his funeral. Anna was in the sixth month of her second pregnancy at the time and wrote her mother that she feared what effect the funeral might have on her [14 September 1880].

For the period of October 1880 to February 1881, another gap exists in the extant correspondence between Anna Stoner and her mother. Most likely, Martha once again lived with Anna through her confinement and the birth of her second child, a son, born just after Christmas, on 28 December 1880, and later named Thomas Royal Stoner.

The Bees Can Hardly Make a Living
January–September 1881

Martha Wellington stayed with Anna about a month following her grandson's birth late in December 1880, and then she returned to her home across the Guadalupe River. On Tuesday, 8 February 1881, while the children napped, Anna wrote Martha that she was feeling well and strong again and that her new son was growing fast. Hope, now twenty-one months old, was also well and reacting positively to the new addition to the family. Anna boasted that Hope "thinks as much of baby brother as she does of kitty & makes as much to do over him as if he *was* kitty." While Anna wrote her mother, she prepared a dinner of "six fried partridges, half a boiled jowl, 'taters, cornbread, and '*lasses* and a nigger to *dine* after us." The meal, representative of contributions made by both Clinton and Anna, was enhanced by the sweet molasses Clinton had purchased from the Venables. The African-American hand who would eat their leftovers was hired to help clear the fields of dead cotton stalks before plowing began. Her confinement period complete, Anna once again was able to go visiting, and Lillie Stoner Hunt came to take Anna to see Mollie Gartrell. At Mollie's Anna also saw Lizzie Stoner, Clinton's aunt, and Lizzie Cunningham, Anna's former schoolmate. In turn, Anna received several visits from Nannie Jordan, who complimented her on Royal's healthfulness, but Anna could not visit with Dora Fromme because three of her children, Anne, Adolph, and Isabell, were ill.

Anna's visits during the early spring were confined to her closest neighbors, however, for she and Clinton were busy planting their year's garden and crops. By the end of the first week of February, Anna had planted one half of her garden in Irish potatoes and the other half in turnips and shallots. Also by that time, Clinton's oats were beginning to come up in the fields, attracting flocks of threatening birds. After Clinton and his hired man cleared the old cotton stalks, Clinton bedded his crop. From the Venables, he purchased seed corn, for which he paid sixty cents a bushel after he himself picked the seed. Clinton abandoned his plowing one day in early February to help a neighbor, an incident Anna shared with her mother in the following narrative:

> Mr. [Joe] J[ordan] sent Mrs. J[ordan] here for Clinton to
> go after Mr. H[ugh] J[ordan] to come & help him to take

> his mill down again, friday evening, it was about to blow
> down again, Clinton went to Mr. H. J.s but he was not at
> home so he went to Mr. Taylors and he stoped his plow as
> Clinton had too & they two helped to take it down, he is
> grinding on it though now but he has to make the tail big-
> ger, it cant hold the wheel in the wind. [8 February 1881]

Jordan's mill was an important asset to his neighbors, and
Clinton and other farmers in the area had a vested interest
in keeping it running, even when doing so meant losing a
day's work.

Although the Stoners lost one cow early in 1881, the rest of
their cattle fared well through the end of winter on the shucks
Clinton fed them, and their hogs found ample forage on their
island pasture. However, the Stoners' horses Charly and Dun
became too sick to complete spring plowing. Their problem was
diagnosed as epizootic, a contagious fungal disease, by one
neighbor, and another neighbor later prescribed a remedy:
pouring a teaspoonful of coal oil down the horses' ears and adding eight grains of green coffee to their feed twice a week. Although Anna confessed to Martha that the treatment "made
Dun deaf for a while," it proved successful eventually [8 February, 24 March 1881].

Busy with housekeeping and gardening through February
and March 1881, Anna waited six weeks before again writing
her mother. Her five-month-old son, Anna related, was "as
good as Hope ever was sometimes I dont touch him but once
between an hour before daylight & dinner & he doenot cry
much I wash him twice or three times a week & a little wipeing
off is all he gets between times." Continuing her boasting,
Anna claimed the baby "is growing very fast & I believe his
eyes are getting gray he laughs & talks to a boddy like he
might have some sense." At this time, Anna told Martha to
record the child's name in the family Bible as Thomas Royal
Stoner, names honoring Clinton's father and brother, both

named Thomas, and also Anna's brother Thomas and her father, Royal Wellington. Anna noted, however, "I expect he will
be called Roy as there is two Tom Stoners." Anna did not
confine her motherly pride to her youngest, but also shared
Hope's latest accomplishments with Martha in the following way:

> Hope is the greatest little busy body you ever saw, tries to
> do every thing she sees us do, she thinks that the chickies,
> kitty, & her 3 kittens & Pinter as she calls him are all
> doubel cousins of hers, she can draw a chair to the table &
> get in it herself, she has been eating by herself ever since
> you left except when there is so many at the table that she
> has not room then I take her in my lap. [24 March 1881]

Near the end of March, the eggs Clinton set in early February hatched, and Anna had almost eighty young chickens to
feed. With feathers in great abundance, Anna hoped to make a
new mattress to replace the one sent from Illinois two years
earlier. She planned to sell that first feather bed to her old
friend Nannie Cromwell Holliday, but, Anna wrote her mother,
Nannie bought instead a new spring mattress at a Victoria
store. Anna had hoped that the sale of the mattress would raise
at least $7.50, the sum required to purchase "a calendar clock
of the Seth Thomas make that Mr. Root sells for 7½ dollars."
Root's price on the clock was a bargain, Anna explained, re-
minding Martha, "You know, J. D. Miller has one that he gave
$16½ for so I thought I'd get that one of Mr. Rs." Since she had
not sold the bed, she would have to be content to wait until the
next fall to make her purchase. "You see," she wrote, "I am
determined to have that kind of clock" [24 March 1881].[17]

In the garden, Anna's English peas were in bloom, and she
had extra mustard greens to share with her neighbors. The
Stoner livestock, however, did not fare as well as their garden.
In addition to the cow lost earlier that year, the Stoners lost a
cow and calf in March 1881. They salvaged the hide from the

cow and sold it to the transient hide buyer who stopped by their farm soon after. Anna reported to Martha that, in spite of their losses, they still had seventeen cattle in all, six cows, eight calves, two two-year-olds, and one three-year-old. In addition to the loss of three head of cattle in 1881, the Stoners lost two colts, both stillborn.

The months of February and March 1881 were unusually dry in Victoria County and news of drought began filtering into Anna's letters. Nevertheless, the Stoners planted their crops successfully and felt confident enough in their outcome to hire John Kay as a field hand for sixteen dollars a month. By the end of March, Clinton had planted five acres of cotton and a few acres of oats. The rest of his land he devoted to raising corn. Charly and Dun, having recovered from epizootic, were "fattening on corn and hard work," Anna wrote her mother. In addition to his own fields, Clinton and his team turned five acres for Joe Jordan in exchange for four bushels of meal. Jordan made the contract with Clinton after having spent a week plowing with his own team and only completing two acres of his dry, packed field. Soon afterwards, when Jordan went to the Venables' farm for seed corn, he told Venable how quickly Clinton and his team had plowed his fields. "Mr. V got on his horse," Anna wrote Martha, "& come down here in hot haste for him to go there to plow so he promised to go today which is Thursday & I am writing by lamp light before daylight & he is on his road there suppose he will do like he did Mr. J wake them up by the dog barking." Drought had hardened Venable's field so severely, however, that Clinton's team alone could not plow the soil. Finally, with four horses hitched to Venable's riding plow, the men completed the job. Venable exclaimed that in all his twenty-five years in Victoria County, his land had never been as hard as it was in the spring of 1881 [24 March 1881].

On Friday, 1 April 1881, the Stoners took a break from their field work, and Anna and her two children accompanied Clinton into town. The purpose of the rare trip, the only visit to Victoria of the entire family recorded in Anna's letters, was to have a family picture taken. The Stoners had six photographs made for various family members so that, as Anna phrased it, "the whole family will go visiting on pasteboard." One picture was for Martha Wellington and one for Thomas, one for Clinton's parents, one for Clinton's sister Mollie Stoner Burt, one for Anna's cousin Augusta Betts Barr, and one for Hawkins and Blanche Cromwell. The photography session did not go well, according to Anna, because just before it began, Hope had been frightened by dogs in the Victoria streets, and she remained upset throughout the visit to town. To make matters worse, Thomas Royal refused to stay still long enough for the slow time exposure required by the camera. Anna hoped that the picture would dispel a rumor circulating among her mother's friends about her physical appearance. In a letter no longer extant, Martha apparently shared the reported gossip with Anna, who responded sharply, writing, "Whoever told you that I had caught cold and was as big as the side of the house & couldn't ware my cloths told a fib & I want them to know it" [4 April 1881].

In addition to having the family picture taken, Clinton Stoner did some shopping while they were all in Victoria. As she later wrote her mother, Anna had asked Clinton to buy enough calico to make three dresses for the children. In the store, however, Clinton discovered that the best quality calico sold in rolls of twelve yards for a dollar. He chose instead to purchase remnants of lawn and batiste, twenty-two yards in all, for a cost of one dollar and eighty cents. Anna admitted that she was "very much pleased" with the finer materials [4 April 1881].

The weather in Victoria County continued dry into mid-April 1881, and then a killing frost hit the lowlands. After the frost, rain finally fell, but it came down in destructive torrents. A stream that ran between the Stoners' and the Frommes' farms

The Stoner Family, 1 April 1881, Victoria, Texas. On left, Anna Louisa Wellington Stoner holds Thomas Royal, age three months. On right, William Clinton Stoner holds Hope Augusta, age twenty-three months. Reproduced by permission of The Texas Collection, Baylor University, Waco, Texas.

had been almost completely dry, Anna reported to Martha, but overnight it filled to the point that it was "swiming to a horse." The frost ruined Clinton's crops and he had just begun replanting when the thunderstorm hit. "Last nights flood stoped all of that for 10 days or more," Anna shared sorrowfully, "so we have a poor show for even corn bread this year." Clinton released his hired man and was, Anna wrote, "in a wors fix now than when he hired him." Anna predicted she and Clinton would have to borrow money to repay a debt at Sibley's gin. Besides contributing to crop failure, the sudden change in weather created health problems among the Stoners and their neighbors. In her late April letter, Anna mentioned to her mother that Hope had contracted chills and fever three successive times, but that each time she had been able to bring the illness under control. The Fromme family, whose children had been too sick earlier in the spring to help in the fields, continued to experience poor health. Even with their own problems, the Stoners were better off than the Frommes, Anna believed. With a touch of irony, she wrote, "Mr. F looks like he would go crazy for if possible he is 'deeper in the mud than we are in the mire' of despondency. How is that for bogging" [26 April 1881]. One year before, Anna had felt a sense of security that inspired her to declare, "Providence has smiled on us in everything" [12 April 1880]. In contrast, April of 1881, with its drought, late freeze, and torrential rain, and the resulting lost crops and ruined health, caused Anna to complain to Martha, "Even the bees can hardly make a living" [26 April 1881].

Perhaps in response to the sad tone of Anna's letter of late April 1881, Martha Wellington decided to pay her daughter a visit in May. Nancy Stoner Cromwell from Fair View and her daughter-in-law, Blanche, who now lived in Tilden, Texas, dropped by Anna's on their way to visit other Stoner relatives in the neighborhood and told Anna that Martha was planning to visit. Hearing of her mother's intent, Anna wrote Martha a quick note on Wednesday, 4 May 1881, which Nancy and

Blanche would carry back to the Wellingtons' home. In a hesitant tone, Anna made the following request:

> Mrs. C[romwell] said that Brother said you wanted to go
> through town to get some little things for the children now
> I dont know whether you intend to get more than some
> little nicknacks or not, but if you do please let one thing be
> a little hat & pr. of shoes for Hope you know I want to go
> to church this summer . . . Now use your own judgement
> you know more about your own affairs than I do so dont
> get the things unless you see fit, no one knows about it
> but my self so dont think you might disappoint me by not
> getting them if it doesnt suit you to do it.

The hat, Anna suggested, could be an inexpensive, plain straw one, costing from ten to fifteen cents, and for trim, she suggested that Martha buy a yard of ribbon for ten cents. Anna estimated the cost of the shoes, which she hoped would be blue or buff, to be fifty to seventy-five cents. For her own needs, Anna anticipated that she herself would be able to purchase a hat and a pair of gaiters, or high-topped shoes, upon selling the chickens she had been raising. With their new hats and their new pairs of shoes, Anna predicted she and Hope would be "pretty well equipt for this neighborhood of aristocracy" [4 May 1881].

Whether or not Martha carried through her visit to the Stoners' home in May and brought Hope the requested accessories remains unknown; however, the next extant letter from Anna to Martha in 1881 followed a trip made by Anna to her mother's. Anna, Hope, and Thomas Royal stayed with Martha during a period when Thomas Wellington traveled to Lockhart and Austin selling horses. Upon returning home, Anna wrote Martha that she found everything there as she had left it, except that "the next morning after we got home Mr. Jordan came down full tilt for Clinton to go for the Dr. & he went too before breakfast." The cause of the excitement, Anna teased, was the birth of "another horrid uggly boy born 11 oclock the 28 of June." Jordan returned to the Stoners' farm a couple of days after his son's birth to borrow their wagon for a trip into Victoria, and Anna asked him to carry her letter to the post office. Along with the letter, Anna sent her mother a package of needles and wished, she wrote, she could send magnesia and paregoric, too, for Martha's health. When she departed Martha's home, Anna had left behind a few dimes for her mother to discover later and to use, she wrote, "to get anything it will buy." Unintentionally, however, she also left behind other things she wanted returned. "I suppose," she wrote, "you have come across Hopes gown by this time. I brought one of those earring loops with me that I was going to put on my hat & left the other one on brothers bed I think." In a bantering tone, Anna continued, "I must have stolen some of your thread dont you miss some? tell Miss Sallie she had better russel around there & russel up my card of buttons if she knows which side of her bread is buttered I bet she has it in her trunk, so now, as Pruny says" [30 June 1881].

Before Martha received Anna's letter of 30 June 1881, she and her housekeeper, Sallie, had discovered the forgotten gown and buttons. Anna realized later that she had not forgotten the earring after all. Martha intended to send the things to Anna, along with a note, by Hezekiah Harvey, the Williamses' hired hand, but only the note reached Anna, because Harvey forgot the bundle. In response to Martha's note, now lost, Anna sat down at the end of the day on the Fourth of July and wrote her mother, saying, "Tell Miss S. I am much obliged to her for finding my things & also to you for mending Hopes gown." She continued by writing, "I suppose you have gotten my letter I wrote to you last week if you havnt I hope the needles in it will stick somebodies fingers." The Stoners had been enjoying eating watermelons, the only successful produce from their garden that summer, and Anna told Martha she had seventeen melons stored under her bed. In her Independence Day letter,

Anna described one way she and Clinton amused themselves during the summer:

> Yesterday we went horseback rideing Clinton took Hope on a pillow & I the baby in my lap we went over to Mrs. J's & Mrs. G's but didnt get down at the latter place then we went to the boyou (I believe that's right) where the stock water, it is a splendid watering place for them.

In the same letter, Anna also recorded her children's weights. At twenty-six months old, Hope weighed twenty-three and a half pounds, and her baby brother, only six months old, already weighed twenty and a half pounds. To secure her family's health during the hot summer months, Anna served milk three times a day, she wrote. She and Clinton decided to forego drinking coffee, saving it for company, and preferred instead to drink peach tea every evening. The benefits of drinking the tea, a tonic she had discovered the previous summer, prompted Anna to exclaim, "oh I do feel so much better." Perhaps to soften the tone of her earlier remarks to Sallie, Anna closed her letter by saying, "Give my love to Miss S & a large share for yourself" [4 July 1881].

On Monday morning, 18 July, Anna put the children down for their morning nap and, before beginning her week's washing, wrote a letter to Martha to thank her for sending by Sallie's brother the things she had left in June. The drought continued into mid-summer, and Clinton cut his parched corn and shocked it for feed. Conditions were so dry, Anna complained, that she could not plant potatoes in the garden for fall. However, on a brighter note, she reported to Martha that she had added some young turkeys to her poultry, and Clinton had traded honey for two new roosters. As the summer heat worsened, the Stoner children had minor fevers, from which they recovered, but when the Jordans' five-year-old son, Harry, became ill, Nannie Jordan wanted to take him to the coast to recover. Anna wrote Martha that she was considering joining Nannie in her trip to

Matagorda Bay, but she wavered in her response: "She wants me to go & Clinton says he would like for me to go to[o] I do not know whether to go or not she thinks she will go next week but I think it doubt full if she will go at all" [18 July 1881]. Anna did not have an opportunity to send her letter of the eighteenth of July to the post office until the thirtieth of that month, and no letter from Anna for the remainder of the summer of 1881 survives to record whether or not she accompanied Nannie Jordan to the coast.

From 1877 to 1881, Anna succeeded in maintaining the overall physical well-being of her husband and children, but she could not devise a remedy for her brother's declining health. Thomas Wellington's illness, diagnosed later as diabetes, progressed rapidly during those years. Although he repeatedly pursued opportunities in the stock business, Thomas did not tolerate well the long hours of exposure to the weather and the rigorous work of driving cattle and horses to market. On every trip he took, he reported feeling ill. For example, in July 1880, he was too weak to return home from Corpus Christi by horseback. He wrote his mother that he had sold his horse to purchase boat fare to Indianola and train fare from Indianola to Victoria, and requested that she send a buggy to meet him at the station to carry him home [5 July 1880]. Realizing his health was worsening, Thomas began investigating climates and sites reputedly healthier than the lowlands. As he traveled into Central Texas during the summer of 1881 selling horses, he looked for a place to relocate. Thomas's search for a healthy environment and less strenuous occupation dominated the remaining three years of his life and became a nagging concern for his sister.

* * * * *

During the first four years of their marriage, Anna and Clinton Stoner gained confidence in their abilities to manage their lives and to cope with most problems that arose. The loss of income during the spring and summer of 1881 caused Clinton to reconsider indebting the family to their landlord for another year's rent. He and Anna had worked from dawn to dusk following the farming cycle of plowing and sowing, but seldom reaping. The Texas coastal soil and climate would not bend to his Midwestern farming techniques. The best economic opportunities in Victoria County now belonged to the large ranchers, and the middle-class farmer had to decide whether to move into town, work for the large ranchers, or move westward.

Clinton concluded that he must try something new, but he did not want to abandon the countryside or to work for someone else. Anna, too, possessed a sense of individualism, which she expressed vividly in her January 1879 letter to Thomas:

> We have all depended too much upon what others said, thought, & did, that has been a *family failing* with us, & being afraid of hurting ourselves at work. I couldn't see it at one time but now I can & have concluded that God hates a fool & lazy person so I have determined not to be either any longer. [21 January 1879]

Anna's strong resolve early in life to put aside dependencies and accept the challenge of self-reliance indicates perhaps an initial shift in personal outlook that would become, later in her life, increasingly less Southern and more frontier in focus. With an independent spirit, the Stoners opted to leave the lowlands of the coastal plain for higher ground in western Texas.

Anna's last extant letter from Victoria County, dated 7 September 1881, gave no hint that she and Clinton planned to move within six weeks. The decision was perhaps an impulsive one, but probably the notion of leaving her lifelong home was of such great concern to Anna that she told her mother about it in person rather than in a letter. The Stoners' willingness to move appears to have been mutual. Anna cast her lot with Clinton and would leave behind her familiar world. Like generations of her family before her, she would travel beyond the margin of settlement into the frontier. The confidence she had gained by coping creatively with her family's needs for housing, food, clothing, and health care in the rural setting of her birth, would soon be tested in a strange and difficult environment.

3
A New Lease On Life

Uvalde County
October 1881–March 1882

Economic and social changes occurring in South Texas during the 1870s echoed those taking place in other agricultural regions throughout the southern United States. Attracted westward by generous land policies and the open range, over four hundred thousand immigrants poured into Texas throughout that decade, pushing the boundary between the farmers' and cattlemen's frontiers ahead of them. Aridity, shallow soil, and lack of transportation halted the farmers' advance into the Edwards Plateau, the southernmost portion of the Great Plains. Located between the Pecos and Colorado rivers and separated from the South Texas Plains by the exposed limestone ridges of the Balcones Escarpment, the plateau held little promise for farmers. Soil suitable for cultivation was found only in a small area in its northeastern section. The remainder of this tableland provided vast grazing areas, the best of which supported cattle; the mediocre, sheep; and the poorest, goats. Surface water was sparse over most of the plateau, but in its southern section among the hills of the escarpment, the headwaters of the Devils, Nueces, Frio, Medina, and Guadalupe rivers rose from the limestone and flowed southward, cutting deep valleys in the mesa before emerging onto the southern plains. Flowing southward through the northwestern quadrant of Uvalde County, the east prong of the Nueces River cut the plateau into steep valleys, called canyons by early Spanish explorers. Large cedar, pecan, elm, and hackberry trees grew near the clear river as it ran swiftly over a rocky bed. Wild game, especially deer and turkey, foraged the native grasses, mesquite, prickly pear, and cactus on the rolling hills.

As the frontier line advanced westward in the 1870s, the lower Nueces River canyon in Uvalde County attracted a small number of pioneers seeking healthful benefits from the clear, pure streams and dry climate. Pioneer farmers entering the area, however, eventually abandoned their attempts to wrest a living from the rocky soil and migrated elsewhere. Ditches dug painstakingly from erratic mountain streams provided the only irrigation, and lack of transportation to markets further inhibited agricultural development. Early cattlemen allowed their Mexican herds to overgraze the already sparse vegetation and soon drove them on to better grasslands. Abandoning the false hope of conquering the wild environs, those pioneers who stayed to become settlers experimented with methods of utilizing the brushy vegetation, abundant water, and steep hills. A few early settlers exploited the natural apiaries formed in caves in the limestone hills and made a living from exporting honey. Others learned to harvest the bat guano in the caves, which they exported to European fertilizer manufacturers.[1] Some settlers acquired sheep herds, but most became raisers of hardy Mexican and Angora goats. The quality mohair of the Angoras, originally imported from Turkey, was highly valued by textile manufacturers. For most canyon settlers, goat raising was a new occupation, often learned by trial and error over a period of years. Although not formally organized, early Angora goat breeders talked among themselves about their work and relied upon one another's experiences. Those families who accommodated well to the demands of their new way of life made a significant contribution to agricultural production in Texas.[2]

News of developments in Uvalde County reached residents of the coastal plains via a long-established military and commercial network that spanned the breadth of South Texas. Refugio County shared economic interests with Uvalde County for almost a decade before Anna Wellington's birth there in 1857. Beginning in the 1840s, steady lines of wagon trains and carts operated westward from St. Mary's on the coast, through Refugio, Goliad, and San Antonio, to Uvalde. At the end of the Civil War, when cattle were overabundant, Uvalde County stock raisers drove their herds two hundred miles east to St. Mary's hide and tallow plants. Also, sheep raisers on the Edwards Plateau exported wool through the busy Aransas Bay port in the early 1870s.[3] Victoria County shared commercial ties with the frontier west of San Antonio from the 1830s, when traders and military personnel began traveling the rugged Chihuahua Trail from Indianola through Victoria, Goliad, and San Antonio to the interior of western Mexico. In the 1840s, German-American immigrants followed the Chihuahua Trail from Indianola to the environs of San Antonio, and fortune-seekers hurried along the military highway west of the Alamo City to Santa Fe on their way to California gold fields. By the end of 1851, stage coaches braved the trail westward, carrying mail and passengers to El Paso.[4] In the 1860s federal troops evacuating West Texas outposts and army headquarters in San Antonio marched the trail eastward to Indianola, then supply wagons for Confederate forces rolled westward into the Texas interior, and finally, federal troops returned westward to their Rio Grande outposts, passing through Indianola and Victoria on their way. After the Civil War, daily stage coaches carried passengers, freight, and mail along the Indianola–Victoria–San Antonio–Uvalde route. Beginning in 1865, fourteen-year-old Prussian immigrant Frederick A. Piper, driving a wagonload of three to four hundred pounds of samples, traveled the rutted trail, bringing goods from Victoria merchants to the scattered pioneers in Uvalde County.[5]

The future of the western fringe of South Texas, however, depended not upon commerce, which advanced continually westward with the railroads, nor upon cattlemen, who moved their herds further west once they had depleted the region's native grasses, but upon its ability to attract permanent settlers. During the decade of 1870–1880 the population of Uvalde County tripled from 851 to 2,541 persons, most of whom made their livings through stock raising, yet the county still had less than two persons per square mile. Unimproved land sold for two to three dollars per acre, and cultivated land rented for the same price; improved land sold for five to eight dollars per acre. Over three hundred sections of state school lands covering 192,999 acres were available in the county at one to two dollars per acre.[6] Although land prices were lower in Uvalde County than in more productive regions, successful stock raising required enormous amounts of acreage. Timber was scarce and expensive, and fencing in Uvalde County in 1882 cost $150 to $250 per mile.[7] With few remaining unexploited resources to attract settlers, the area promoted its climate as its primary asset. In an article originally addressed to the *San Antonio Herald* and later reprinted in an 1879 almanac, an anonymous Uvalde resident recommended Uvalde to all "capitalists . . . and readers looking in this direction for health, homes and happiness." Uvalde, the author boasted, was "the sanitine sunshine-cream-and-honey of Western Texas" with its "vastly superior grazing country, unrivaled in climate and practically illimitable in point of range." Another almanac, published three years later, reported the mean temperature of the county to be eighty-five degrees in summer and forty-five in winter and the mountains in the northwest corner of the county to be especially beneficial to persons with pulmonary disease.[8]

The promise of improved health was the principal factor in attracting Clinton and Anna Stoner from the lowlands of the coastal plains to the hills of the Nueces River canyon. The culmination of a year of drought and disease prompted the young couple to listen favorably to reports of the salutary climate of the Edwards Plateau. Also, the Stoners heard enticing stories related by Victoria County cattlemen who, forced by drought to look for new pastures, had discovered the advantages of the open grasslands west of San Antonio. As the Stoners traveled westward from Victoria County in 1881, their personal way of life changed forever just as Texas and the entire nation were undergoing permanent changes created by the advance of the railroads and the subsequent transformation of the western frontier.

Anna Louisa Stoner continued writing regular letters throughout her journey westward and upon her arrival in Uvalde County. The last extant letter written by Anna from Victoria County before her move related news to Martha Wellington of the children's health and of ways Clinton and neighboring farmers helped one another gather and haul corn and cut hay. Anna also wrote Martha that Clinton and a friend wanted to "go up the country to look out horses," but, Anna claimed, " 'we women folks' persuaded them not to go this fall as they will have a great deal to do & wouldn't have time to see much if they went before they would have to come back again" [7 September 1881]. Whether or not Anna tried to dissuade Clinton from moving in the manner in which she had prevented his trip to round up horses remains unknown. The next extant correspondence from Anna, a penny postcard, sent from Goliad on Saturday, 22 October, told of the successful start of the family's journey the previous Tuesday. For the next month, Anna wrote one or two cards each week informing her mother about her progress across South Texas. In all, she sent six cards from the post offices she passed on her journey: Goliad, Panna Maria, San Antonio, Castroville, Sabinal, and Uvalde. After arriving in the lower Nueces River canyon on 10 November, Anna wrote longer letters describing her new physical surroundings and the family's adjustment to life in southwest Texas. Twice a week a mail rider traveled from Montell, the nearest post office, to Uvalde, thirty miles south, in an open buggy, sometimes carrying passengers and freight along with the mail. William Jones, with whom the Stoners lived when they first arrived in the canyon, provided livery for the mail rider, so the Joneses and Stoners were the first families in the canyon to receive their mail upon the rider's return from Uvalde each Tuesday and Saturday. Nine letters and one postcard which Anna wrote and sent with the mail rider to Uvalde during the five months between November 1881 and March 1882 survived to the present. Anna addressed eight of the letters and the postcard to Martha Wellington and one letter to Thomas Wellington. Four extant letters sent Anna by her mother and one sent by her brother informed the Stoners of events back in Victoria County. In addition to her own nearest relatives, Anna wrote Clinton's parents in Illinois. On Christmas Eve 1881, Thomas Chilton Stoner, Clinton's father, arrived in the Nueces River canyon to visit his son and meet his daughter-in-law and grandchildren for the first time. Then, in February 1882, Thomas Wellington made the journey to Uvalde County to see for himself the place his sister described so carefully in her letters. Two letters written by Nancy Hathaway Stoner to Anna during Nancy's husband's visit to the canyon and one written by Thomas Wellington to his mother giving his first impressions of the region shed further light on the Stoner family's new way of life in the west.

In her letters from the Nueces River canyon, Anna expressed for the first time a strong sense of place. No record exists indicating whether Anna or her mother ever traveled westward beyond Victoria and Refugio counties before the autumn of 1881. Thomas Wellington drove horses to Lockhart and Austin the previous summer, but Clinton Stoner probably never traveled that far west into Texas before 1881. Because she was entering places and seeing sights she had never before encountered, Anna took great care in her letters to recreate those experiences for her mother. As long as she lived in the region of her birth and childhood, Anna did not describe the physical environs beyond her house and farm. The location of her third home, designated in letters with the words *At home* rather than by the name of the nearest post office, is determinable only from census records and contemporary memoirs. The farther she traveled westward from her birthplace, however, the more Anna wrote about the surrounding topography, vegetation, animal life, and climate. Perhaps Anna's growing sense of place reflected feelings of liberation as she left behind the relatively restrictive, highly organized society of Victoria County for the less restrained, less structured environment of Uvalde County. Or, perhaps the coarseness of her new physical setting engendered feelings of estrangement, and by formulating words about the minute details of her surroundings, Anna hoped to establish a sense of order in the wilderness.[9] Whatever her unconscious motive, Anna's avowed reason for giving detailed accounts of the land and resources of Uvalde County was to answer the questions she knew her mother, brother, and in-laws would have concerning the Stoner family's new home. Anna hoped that wherever she and Clinton settled, Martha and Thomas Wellington would eventually join them. Although she admitted to her mother that she did not "really like this country as far as looks are concerned," Anna invited the Wellingtons

to "come up here all the same & we will help each other &
all live together in one family & be happy" [4 December 1881].
While she also wanted Clinton's father to visit South Texas,
she did not want him to make the long trip from Illinois with
false expectations of what he would find. Therefore, putting
into practice the lessons learned during her schooldays in writing letters filled with the details of everyday experience, Anna
sought to describe for her father-in-law as candidly as she could
her new setting and changed way of life. Anna explained the
method of her description in a later letter to her mother as follows:

> I got a letter from Clinton's mother Saturday too; she
> beged me to ans. it immediately to his Pa as he is crazy to
> come out here again so yesterday I wrote him an 8 page
> one the size of this paper told him all about the country
> that I knew & more too, told him that if he found it differ-
> ent when he came that he could attribute it to his not see-
> ing through my eyes, so now I think that letter will either
> bring him here or else he will stay at home. I told him all
> about how we were living, what kinds of dishes we had, &
> every thing else I could of. [12 December 1881]

The major themes of Anna's cards and letters from the time
she left Victoria County in October 1881 to the time she and
Clinton located land to buy in Edwards County in March 1882
were the journey itself, the environment they entered, and the
ways the family adjusted to its temporarily unsettled condition.
Each letter during the journey mentioned improvements made
in the family's health as they drew farther away from the lowlands. Also woven throughout the letters of this period is the
Stoners' search for a place to settle and for a means of making a
living. The decision-making process shared by Anna and
Clinton illustrate the maturation of their marriage during a period of vast change in their lives.

Good Health and Good Spirits
18 October–10 November 1881

On Tuesday, 18 October 1881, Clinton and Anna Stoner and their children, Hope Augusta, aged two and a half years, and Thomas Royal, aged ten months, left Victoria County, Texas, in a wagon filled with their most valued farming implements and household furnishings. Before leaving, they sold their cattle, hogs, and poultry. Anna made room on the wagon for her sewing machine, but left behind her heavy stove. Along with the Stoners traveled the family of William and Mattie Lynn Jones, former neighbors of Martha and Thomas Wellington at Anaqua. William and Mattie Jones and their son Clarence had migrated by 1874 to the Texas coast from South Carolina. In Victoria County, they added four daughters and a son to their family: Leila, twins Fannie and Ellen, Virginia, and Lynn. Like the Wellingtons and Cromwells, the Joneses were Presbyterians, and the families may have met when the circuit preacher came to Anaqua to hold home services.[10] Another connection also linked the Stoners and the Joneses. In 1874 Clinton Stoner's cousin, Maria, daughter of Michael Lowery Stoner, married Richard Lynn, the brother of Mattie Lynn Jones. Richard Lynn's first wife, Laura, who died in South Carolina soon after their marriage, was the sister of William Jones, Mattie's husband. In 1875 Richard and Maria Stoner Lynn had a daughter, whom they named Laura. Two years later, Lynn, a lawyer by profession, died of consumption at the age of twenty-eight.[11] His widow and daughter lived in the ranch compound of the Stoner Pasture Company and often visited "Cousin Clint" and his wife, Anna, in their home across the Guadalupe River. Maria and Laura Lynn either accompanied the Joneses and Stoners to Uvalde County or joined them a few weeks later, for when Anna wrote her mother on 1 December 1881 from the Nueces River canyon, Maria was with the Jones family, with whom Anna and her children also lived while Clinton looked for land to buy or rent. For several years, Maria and Laura traveled between the Joneses' ranch near Montell and the Stoner Pasture Company near Kemper's Bluff, visiting their relatives for many months at a time.

When Clinton and Anna Stoner left Victoria County for Uvalde County in the fall of 1881, they followed the mail and stage route through Goliad, Helena, and Panna Maria to San Antonio. From there they took the old military road through Castroville and D'Hanis to Uvalde. Upon leaving Victoria County, the Stoner and Jones wagons stopped first in Goliad. Several days of rain made the road impossible to travel, and the families found refuge in a vacant house. On Saturday, 22 October, Anna sent a postcard to her mother stating that "all are well & in good spirits" [22 October 1881]. While in Goliad, the Stoners washed the mud from their clothes and wagons and repaired their tent. The rainy weather may have prevented Anna from attending the Presbyterian Church in Goliad, led by W. E. Caldwell, who performed her wedding ceremony four years earlier. In Goliad in 1881, the Stoners were probably aware of the ruins of "Old Town" at the historic site of Presidio Nuestra Señora de Loreto and Mission La Bahiá del Espíritu Santo de Zúñiga, across the San Antonio River and two miles south of the "New Town." They were likely more impressed, however, with Goliad's county courthouse, churches, hotels, military academy, and rock homes.[12] When they entered Goliad County, the Stoners began traveling through increasingly well-settled and developed country. As they traveled westward, they passed through towns that were on the verge of changes that would affect their future permanently. Depending on the route followed by the railroads, some of the towns would prosper and some would decline within the next decade.

On Monday, 24 October 1881, the Stoner and Jones wagons departed Goliad and followed the stage route along the San Antonio River to Helena, at that time the county seat of

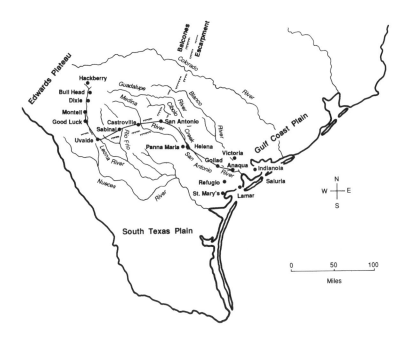

South Texas 1881. Detail of route of Stoner family migration 1881. Adapted from A. W. Spaight, *The Resources, Soil, and Climate of Texas* (Galveston, TX: A. H. Belo, 1882). Inset map locates area of Texas covered by larger map.

Karnes County. Midpoint on the Chihuahua Trail between Indianola and San Antonio, Helena once served as an important resting place for antebellum traders who drove solid-wheeled oxcarts laden with merchandise from northern Mexico to the Gulf Coast. Later, it became a major station on the stage line connecting San Antonio and the coast. By the time the Stoners and Joneses passed through Helena in 1881, the town had a rock courthouse, private academy, church, two hotels, boot shop, harness shop, livery stable, and numerous saloons, to serve a population of three hundred. The Stoners crossed the San Antonio River at Helena on an iron bridge recently built to replace the toll bridge used since the town's early days. A few years after the Stoners stopped in Helena, the tracks of the San Antonio and Aransas Pass Railroad bypassed the town and the population dwindled permanently. Karnes City replaced Helena as the county seat in the 1890s.[13]

The travelers lingered in Helena until Friday, 28 October, because of continuing rain and muddy roads. When the rains ended, they took a day to sun their belongings before commencing their journey. A few miles west of Helena, at the confluence of the San Antonio River and Cibolo Creek, the Stoners and Joneses stopped at the village of Panna Maria, where on Saturday, 29 October, Anna wrote her mother a second postcard to report "all [are] well & in fine roads for once" [29 October 1881]. Panna Maria, the first permanent Polish settlement in America, had seventy families in 1877, when they began building the imposing Church of Immaculate Conception of the Blessed Virgin Mary. Since 1851, stage coaches had stopped in Panna Maria on their way from Indianola to San Antonio. In 1884, however, the San Antonio and Aransas Pass Railroad bypassed the village, just as it did Helena, and Panna Maria thereafter remained a small community of related families. [14]

From Panna Maria, the Stoner and Jones families drove their wagons along the stage road through the towns of Floresville,

Sutherland Springs, and Lavernia in Wilson County and Saint Hedwig in eastern Bexar County before reaching San Antonio about eight o'clock on Thursday morning, 3 November 1881. Just before reaching the wagon yard where they would camp overnight, one of the Joneses' wagon wheels broke. While the men repaired the wheel, Anna wrote a card to her mother giving her first impressions of the city whose history dated from the Spanish mission period. In 1881 San Antonio was in the midst of a decade of growth that began with the coming of the Sunset Route of the Galveston, Harrisburg, and San Antonio Railroad in 1877. The rail lines created a market connection for Texas stock raisers, and multitudes of cattle drovers frequently gathered at saloons and gambling halls in the city. For the Mexican residents, cock-fighting was the most popular sport.[15] On her first day in San Antonio, Anna wrote Martha that she had decided that it was "the crookedest town" she had ever seen because "cocks & business & faro is the order of the day here" [3 November 1881].

After Anna saw more of the city, she concluded that it had a better side. The day she left San Antonio, Anna wrote Martha from Castroville, claiming, "We saw a good deal of San A[ntonio], all of which was pleasing" [4 November 1881]. In addition to cattle drovers, the rails brought immigrants seeking permanent homes, and by 1881, San Antonio, with a population of over twenty thousand, had its first streetcars, gas lights, and telephones. Also, by 1881, the United States Army had established Post San Antonio, later known as Fort Sam Houston, and a second rail line, the International and Great Northern, began serving the city.[16] Two weeks after leaving the historic city, Anna reflected in a letter to Martha that "San Antonio is a beautiful place & I would love to live there if I was able." Anna thought the San Antonio River was "beautiful," and "doesn't look like the same river of our acquaintance down there at the mouth." The bridge across the river and the "fine" houses on its banks also attracted Anna's attention [16 November 1881].

Besides memories of both the rough and refined social sides of San Antonio, the Stoners carried to Uvalde souvenirs of their visit. Anna and Clinton arranged to have a photograph taken of their children while they were in town, but they had difficulty getting Hope to cooperate for the sitting, just as they had previously in Victoria. Anna later explained what had transpired to her mother:

> When we were at San Antonio we had the babies picture taken & tried our best to get Hope but she cried so we couldn't; nothing we could do would prevent her crying, apples, candy, doll or any thing else wouldn't induce her to sit for it . . . I sat by her but that would do no good then we tried the baby & got three like this one . . . then we tried Hope again but it was just the same as before I didn't feel like haveing his without hers it didn't seem right. [16 November 1881]

Also, before they left the city, Anna and Clinton bought Hope and Thomas matching chairs with rawhide seats, in which were punched the first initial of each child's name. Clinton secured the chairs in the wagon and the children rode on them all the way to the Nueces River canyon.[17]

When the Stoner and Jones families departed San Antonio on Friday, 4 November 1881, they crossed the ninety-eighth meridian that for several decades had separated the settled areas of South Texas from the frontier. They followed the military road twenty-five miles west to Castroville, where they spent the weekend. Along their journey, the Stoners and Joneses traveled slowly to prevent injury to their horses and to accommodate the needs of eight young children. They did not travel on Sundays, but rested, following the Christian practice of keeping the Sabbath. On Sunday, 6 November, in Castroville, the Stoners probably witnessed the gathering of the townspeople at St. Louis Catholic Church, which housed the headquarters of the Sisters of Divine Providence, or at the town's Lutheran church. The Catholic and Lutheran churches remained the only denominations organized into churches in the former Alsatian colony for one hundred years, a fact that led one historian to describe Castroville as "a French town with a German flavor growing out of Texas soil."[18] Just prior to the Stoners' visit to their town, the 159 families of Castroville voted against granting a bonus that would have brought the railroad through their town. When the train tracks bypassed the town and commerce ceased along the Chihuahua Trail, Castroville dwindled in importance. In 1892, the town of Hondo, situated on the Southern Pacific line, became the seat of Medina County government, replacing Castroville.

From Castroville, Anna wrote Martha that she could see mountains in the distance and that, whereas the grass between Victoria County and San Antonio was "very short," they now entered an area of high grass and "passed fields of wheat stubble & stacks of straw." Anna claimed that as they moved farther and farther from the lowlands everyone who began the journey ill grew healthier and that her babies were "fat and saucy" [4 November 1881]. By Wednesday, 9 November, the wagons reached the hills of the Sabinal canyon in eastern Uvalde County. Camping beside the Sabinal River, Anna again wrote her mother, saying, "We are nearly to our journeys end now & are up here among the mountains in a pretty place. . . . We are all well & getting fat" [9 November 1881]. A new railway station in the village of Sabinal awaited the completion of the Mexican and Pacific extension of the Galveston, Harrisburg, and San Antonio Railroad. Just beyond Sabinal, the Stoners noted crews laying rails that would reach Uvalde two months later, in January 1882. In her card mailed from Sabinal, Anna requested that Thomas Wellington check on mail addressed to her and Clinton that may have collected in the

Victoria post office. She particularly wanted to receive the November and December issues of *Gleanings* and *The Household*. Clinton, she reported, had gathered some newspapers and magazines from the post office before they began their journey, and, apparently, Anna passed much of the time on the slow-moving wagon reading and rereading her favorite periodicals. Although her living conditions on the trail were far different from her small, but well-filled, rural farmhouse in Victoria County, Anna maintained a lively interest in domesticity.

On Thursday, 10 November 1881, the Stoner and Jones families briefly visited the town of Uvalde, seat of Uvalde County government. When Anna Stoner first saw Uvalde, the town of about eight hundred inhabitants was on the eve of permanent change. Settled in 1853 by Reading Wood Black and Nathan L. Stratton near Leona Station on the Chihuahua Trail, Uvalde remained on the western edge of the Texas frontier until the railroad reached there in January 1882. A year after Anna witnessed the laying of tracks less than twenty miles east of town, the rail line through Uvalde became part of the vast Southern Pacific Railroad extending from New Orleans to San Francisco. The coming of the railroads to southwestern Texas spelled the demise of the Chihuahua Trail as a primary commercial and mail route. As an important way station on the old trail for cattlemen and Mexican traders, the village of Uvalde earned a reputation for lawlessness, and during the Civil War the entire county fell under the domination of Comanches and Apaches. In the late 1870s and early 1880s, the village became a town, as settlers pushed westward into the area, and signs of organized community appeared in Uvalde: churches, schools, newspapers, general mercantile stores, a new courthouse, and a volunteer fire department. When she wrote her mother from Uvalde in November 1881, Anna noted that two doctors served the town, but because people living there were so healthy, "one keeps sheep & the other, a store for a living." During the single day the Stoners and Joneses spent in Uvalde, Clinton visited a surveyor to learn the locations of available land in the lower Nueces River canyon, thirty miles northwest of town, which he knew to be "the Canion that [Charlie] McF[addin] lives at" [10 November 1881]. McFaddin, a rancher from drought-stricken Victoria County, preceded the Stoners into Uvalde County to lease pasture from John R. Baylor. Eager to complete their journey, the Stoners and Joneses set out for the canyon that same day, reaching a campsite that evening along the banks of Montell Creek "within walking distance of McF's place on land that belongs to a General Baler" [16 November 1881].

Anna and Clinton Stoner completed the journey of approximately 254 miles from their farm in Victoria County to the lower Nueces River canyon in twenty-three days. Traveling slowly and deliberately, the Stoners and their companions, the Joneses, experienced only minor mishaps on the way: a few days' delay caused by muddy roads, one broken wagon wheel, and the loss of two of the Stoners' kittens. For all but the last thirty miles of the trip, the wagons followed well-traveled roads through settled rural areas, with towns and villages spaced at regular intervals. Anna missed her mother and brother, but loneliness was not a predominant theme of her move west. The Stoners journeyed with familiar people who shared their values and hopes, and they expected to find acquaintances waiting for them upon reaching their destination. The least comfortable part of the journey came at its end on the rugged wagon track leading north from Uvalde, which wound through the rising slopes of the Balcones Escarpment and crossed and recrossed the meandering Nueces River. Almost a week after they finally reached their destination at Montell Creek, Anna wrote Martha: "This part of the cannion is very pretty, but we thought of all the God forsaken places on earth the part we came over to get here was the worst" [16 November 1881].[19]

During the five months the Stoner family lived in northwestern Uvalde County, the young couple faced myriad decisions, the greatest of which were where to live and how to make a living. In addition to advice given by established settlers in the canyon, they received suggestions proposed by their parents about where and how they should live. Anna left the final decision to Clinton, but her letters indicate that she participated fully in the process. The journey and subsequent months of unsettledness, combined with the mutual need to prove their independence, created a sense of partnership between Anna and Clinton. As she observed Clinton's investigations of the pros and cons of settling in the canyon, Anna herself gained skills in problem-solving and self-reliance that would prove valuable the rest of her life.

Waters Clear as Crystal
November–December 1881

Four elements of the lower Nueces River canyon environment stood out in the mind of Anna Stoner as she described in letters how the canyon differed from her former home on the flat coastal prairie in Victoria County: the mountains, the water, the wildlife, and the people. Although she claimed to dislike what she saw, Anna's imagery painted a distinctly positive picture for her mother and brother. Having lived all her life on the near-sea-level plains of the Texas Gulf Coast, Anna considered the hills of the Balcones Escarpment "mountains." Visible in the distance from the prairie the Stoners traversed on their way into the Nueces River canyon, the brushy slopes rose to elevations between one and two thousand feet. While camping in the canyon valley alongside Montell Creek, Anna described for her mother the sensation of being among the mountains: "You can't stand in one place & look over miles of country as this is timbered, unless you are on a mountain side then you

can see every thing as far as the eye can reach & see where
your stock is too." A week after their arrival in the canyon,
Anna walked to the top of "one of the hi[gh]est mountains of
the range." Anna claimed, "I was so high that grown cattle and
horses in the valley looked like they were the size of goats &
when I look[ed] directly down it would make my head swim.
Clinton pulled me half the way up or I would never have goten
up to the top" [16 November 1881]. Later, writing Thomas
Wellington, Anna compared the mountains and the plains:

> Though I do not really *like* this country as far as *looks* are
> concerned still I think it has many advantages over that &
> 'vise versa' (now you lattin scholar, I don't know whether
> that is spelt right or not) we are surrounded by mountains
> & you cant see the sun rise & set, as it rises & sets behind
> mountains, & you know we come from a prearie country &
> *here* we cant see for the brushes the mountains instead of
> being covered with trees is covered with grass, rocks,
> brush, catsclaw, pricly-pare, dagger choto or soto or what-
> ever they call it with cedar breaks & timber between
> them—the mountains—with plats of grass everywhere.
> Creeks run down between the mountains & emty in the
> river on each side of the creeks such vallies are good
> places for stock of any kind to winter in, & summer too, if
> water lasts. [4 December 1881]

In addition to the mountains, the Nueces River and the
creeks that flowed into it dominated Anna's first impressions
of the lower canyon. Although she grew up beside the San Antonio River and later lived near the Guadalupe River, Anna realized immediately that near its headwaters, the Nueces River
was nothing like the slow, muddy waters near the Gulf Coast.
Originating about thirty miles north of Montell in Edwards
County, the east prong of the Nueces River flowed swiftly
southward through the rocky canyon, occasionally returning
underground. Hundreds of creeks and streams fed the river,

111

and a heavy rainfall upstream meant certain flooding downstream. Anna described the canyon water supply to her mother with precise imagery:

> The water is spring, creek, well, and river, which is all as clear as cristall, we campt near the bank of Montell Creek; in some places you can walk over on dry gravel for yards at such places the water runs *under* the gravel instead of over it. here at the camp it is 3 or 4 ft. deep but you can see the bottom *so* plain that you would think it was very shallow we can see the perch & trout swimming as plain as if they were in a glass cage when they are near the bottom. the river dries up in summer to only pools here & there in it, but still they say it is enough for stock—the creeks dry entirely up in summer.

Along the river bottom grew trees familiar to Anna: cottonwood, cypress, oak, cedar, and pecan. The abundance of native pecan groves along the Nueces had inspired its name, the Spanish word for "nut." Besides enjoying the beauty of the water, canyon settlers had learned to use to advantage the fact that, as Anna discovered, "the water in these streams & springs is warm in winter and cold in summer." Those families who milked cows ran the spring water through their dairies, Anna reported to Martha, "so as to keep their milk sweet almost any length of time" [16 November 1881]. In late November, Thomas wrote Anna that the people in the lowlands had just experienced a cold spell, the first portent of winter. In reply, Anna wrote her brother that the canyon folk had likewise felt the change in weather, but there the temperature fell low enough to create a "white frost" and to freeze the campers' drinking water, stored in buckets hung from tree limbs. Even though the temperature fell lower in Uvalde County than in Victoria County, the higher, drier atmosphere there felt less cold than the humidity-laden climate of the coast. Anna explained to Thomas, "It turns warm here as it does there between northers but still we do not feel the cold as much." Anna recorded metaphorically for Thomas the effects of the cold winter atmosphere upon the warm water: "The water in the creek those mornings was nearly milk warm & a steam rose from it like your breath on a cold day" [4 December 1881].

In the canyon, the Stoners found abundant game, which, along with fish, became their primary sources of protein while they camped. On 19 November, Anna boasted to Martha, "Wild turkeys are plentifull. Clinton killed 7 seven day before yesterday & a few days before that Mr. J[ones] & him killed two. so you see turkeys are the order of the day here" [16 November 1881]. Completely new to Anna was the proximity of bears to the canyon. Canyon settlers told Clinton that bears were abundant in the mountains about twenty or twenty-five miles distant. The previous winter, the Baylor family killed eleven bears and rendered bear fat into lard in the manner used for hog fat. Newcomers Stoner and Jones decided to see the bears for themselves and, late in November, joined their neighbors on a bear hunt. In her letter written to Martha on the first of December, Anna reported that Clinton had no opportunity to shoot a bear on his trip because his horse could not keep up with the other horses on the hilly inclines. His companions killed bear, however, and for the first time the Stoners had "some genuine bear steak." During the hunt, the temperature suddenly fell below freezing, and at nightfall, the men sought shelter in one of the numerous limestone caves in the region. Clinton, not expecting the sudden norther, had no coat with him on the hunt, and so he slept on his saddle blanket by the fire at the mouth of the cave. Although he did not return to camp with bear meat, Clinton brought back something he probably liked better: honey robbed from a natural apiary in the cave where he spent the night [1 December 1881]. About the time of Clinton's experience in the mountain cave, Thomas Wellington, back in Victoria County, wrote Anna and mentioned that when he had told Francis Hawkins Cromwell about the Stoners' move to Uvalde County, Cromwell predicted that Clinton would "dance himself to death over the bee caves" [29 November 1881].

Rough living conditions were common to all early settlers in the lower canyon and contributed to a democratic spirit within the small community. Some neighbors lived "close together," Anna observed to Martha, but others were "3, 4, 5, & 6 miles apart." Within the first week of their arrival, five women visited Anna and Mattie Jones, and Anna expected more to come. Among the first visitors were Mrs. John R. Baylor and her son, with his wife and children. The Baylors, originally from Kentucky, received a league of Nueces River canyon land from the state of Texas in recognition of General Baylor's military service and moved into the area in 1878. Baylor bought the land grants of other former soldiers and soon amassed ten thousand acres, three of which he donated for a church, school, and cemetery in the community he named Montell, for the original surveyor of the region, Charles de Montel. Baylor also helped organize a unit of home guards, which Anna called "a minit company," to protect settlers from renegade Indians, who occasionally stole horses in the canyon.[20]

When the Baylors and other settlers visited the Stoners and Joneses, the conversation revolved around concerns common to both settlers and new arrivals: health, living arrangements, and stock and land prices. Anna received frequent assurance that in the canyon "every one seems to have a new leace of life." Like the newcomers, earlier settlers had come seeking improved health and were not disappointed. Anna wrote her mother that they claimed to "never have pneumonia or anything else." Although settlers in the canyon were thirty miles from the nearest doctor, they claimed no one in the lower canyon had died from poor health, and Anna told Martha, "I can't tell you how people die here as they say that they are never sick" [16 November 1881]. As for the Stoners, Anna assured her mother, "We all feel so much better than we generaly do at this season of the year, & the children: the blood seems ready to burst out of their faces" [1 December 1881]. To Thomas, she exclaimed, "I believe this is as healthy a place as ever was made" [4 December 1881].

The more experienced women in the canyon recognized the apprehensions Anna Stoner and Mattie Jones felt about leaving the secure shelter of houses to live in tents. From her visitors, Anna learned that she had a lot in common with her new neighbors, for, as she wrote Thomas, "everyone here has camped & lived in a tent & many are not much better off yet" [4 December 1881]. Timber for building houses was scarce in the canyon, and Anna discovered that most of the houses in the area were made of cedar posts, and a few from lumber, and their interior walls were lined with a limestone mixture "as white as plaster of paris." The more experienced settlers also shared food with the Stoners and Joneses, giving them portions of surplus game and dairy products. From the Baylor's spring-cooled dairy, Anna wrote Martha, came "buttermilk that is almost sweet."

In the three years prior to the Stoners' arrival in the lower Nueces River canyon, earlier settlers began introducing the amenities of organized society. They established a Methodist church at Montell, where, they told Anna when she arrived, they hoped a minister surnamed Wools, formerly of Victoria, would become their pastor. Anna recalled for her mother that Wools once faced charges of drunkenness in the church in Victoria but received an acquittal. Another preacher familiar to Anna, J. Zibley, was pastor of a church in Uvalde and preached at Montell once a month. Zibley, Anna remembered, organized the church at Kemper's Bluff in Victoria County. Among settlers and newcomers in the area, Anna found "no Mexicans or negrows." According to Anna, frequent parties occurred for the benefit of the young men and women. Among the Montell area settlers, who in the 1880 census numbered 242 persons, Anna found numerous young people, including "some of the

pretiest girls Clinton says he ever saw" [16 November 1881].[21]
The church, the minute company, the visits, and the socials,
and the fact that Montell also had a school, all fortified Anna's
eventual claim to Martha that even in the remoteness of the
Nueces River canyon, her family was "not entirely out of the
world" [25 December 1881].

When experienced settlers visited newcomers to the canyon,
the conversation inevitably turned to the matters uppermost in
their minds: stock and land. Before committing their savings to
buying either, newcomers had to know whether or not they
could make a living from their investments. As soon as they
set up camp near Charlie McFaddin's place on Montell Creek,
Clinton Stoner and William Jones visited John R. Baylor, on
whose land they camped. Anna reported to her mother that the
men regarded Baylor as "one of the old Kentucky gentlemen,"
and they learned from him that cattle and goats survived in
the canyon brush better than sheep. Baylor had some "Cassim-
ear" goats, Anna claimed, perhaps referring to Angoras. She
reported to her mother that Baylor considered the long-haired
goats advantageous because the raisers "can have any goat
hides dressed here & sell them for nearly as much as the common goat costs, besides having the meat & suet left." Anna understood the diversified grazing habits that allowed cattle and
goats to share the same area, which she stated in simple terms:
"the goats eat the brush and the cattle the grass which is very
abundant and fine" [16 November 1881]. Browsing goats destroyed small shrubs and pruned bushes and trees up to four or
five feet, thereby clearing an area in which grass could flour-
ish. After grass replaced the brush, stock raisers moved cattle
into the area. From Baylor's wife and sons, the Stoners learned
the cost of milk cows in the canyon. Although the cows were
common Mexican cattle, Anna knew they produced good milk
and butter, because the Baylors shared some with them. But
milk cows were few and cost more than better bred dairy cattle
in Victoria. The price of a cow with calf in the canyon ranged

from thirty to thirty-five dollars. Throughout her first five months' stay in Uvalde County, Anna had no cows to milk, no chickens to feed, and no garden to tend. She cooked her family's meals over a campfire and washed their clothes in the river.

Clinton and Anna also learned from established settlers where available land was and what it cost. Upon first arriving in the canyon, the Stoners discovered that those ahead of them had already purchased most of the land around Montell, including, Anna exclaimed to Martha, "land that looks as if it wouldn't feed a goose to the acre" [16 November 1881]. During his first week in the canyon, Clinton began checking reports about land north of Montell. He visited a tract of fourteen hundred acres for sale for one thousand dollars and some less expensive state school land. As he became better acquainted with the land and talked to more experienced stock raisers, Clinton decided to lease or rent land at the current rate of two to three cents per acre rather than buy, investing the majority of his capital in sheep rather than land. Land was cheap and easy to get, but sheep were in demand and their price was escalating. Anna wrote her brother about her husband's plan:

> Clinton is going to buy sheep with a part of our money & put the other at interest so if any thing *should* happen to the sheep we would have some thing to fall back on then he will leace land & either live in a house shaped tent or one that might be on the land, he dose not think it would pay to put half or nearly half of our money in a place that we could not make a liveing on without stock the wealthiest men here lease their land or most of it & move their stock to the range as the range changes.

Clinton recognized his decision to keep sheep might not meet the approval of area cattlemen, who often looked unfavorably upon renting out their land for sheep pasture. Anna explained to Thomas that owners would allow any size herd of cattle on

117

their land, but *"sheep men are obliged to herd their sheep on the land that they control* as cattle dislike to grase after them" [4 December 1881]. In order to control his herd, Clinton learned that he should look for land along one of the hundreds of creeks in the canyon, where he could keep his sheep on the hills and settle his family in the valley at the mouth of the creek. After looking for land in the lower Nueces River canyon for one month and not locating any he wanted to buy, Clinton Stoner leased land from fellow newcomer William Jones and put on it four hundred dollars' worth of sheep. His venture proved successful; he kept his first sheep herd two months and sold them for a two hundred dollar profit.

By the first of December, the Joneses had located land and a house to rent. Anna complained to Martha that Clinton would have taken the same land "had it not been that Mr. J. first saw & bargained for this place" [1 December 1881]. The Stoners' search for a place to live included locating adjacent land for Martha and Thomas Wellington, thereby limiting their choices in the lower canyon and lengthening the time it took to find a site. Almost every one of Anna's early letters from Uvalde County mentioned her expectation that Martha and Thomas Wellington would soon join her. Letters to Anna from her mother and brother also expressed their eagerness for the Stoners to locate land so that they could decide whether or not they, too, would move to the canyon. The Wellingtons were in a state of uncertainty after Anna's departure from Victoria County, and their letters exerted sometimes subtle, sometimes overt pressure on the young couple to settle quickly. A week after the Stoners began their journey to Uvalde, the Wellingtons' close friend and neighbor, David F. Williams, died. Thomas Wellington wrote his sister about Williams's death, whom, he said, he had considered like a father. In order to be near her widowed friend during her period of mourning, Martha moved into Amanda Williams's home. Thomas sold her former home, adjacent to the Williams's farm, and moved into another nearby house, rented from Francisco Ticerino. Both mother and son expected to leave Victoria County soon. Thomas further reported to Anna that after her departure, their mother underwent a period of despondency. Martha wanted to spend the winter with Anna and Clinton, wherever they settled, but she was not yet ready for Thomas to leave her to visit the canyon to determine whether she should make the trip. Thomas explained to his sister, "She is afraid that she might die when we are both away, and is terribly afraid that she will never see you or the babies again" [29 November 1881]. As more and more wagonloads of families entered the lower Nueces River canyon, Anna and Clinton worried that the region would become overcrowded, resulting in escalated land and stock costs. In writing to her brother in early December, Anna urged him to encourage their mother "to not drag her feet" but make a decision about moving to the canyon before favorable economic conditions there ended. Anna softened her imperative, with a confession of doubt, writing:

> Oh Brother I don't know what to do. I want you all here so much & yet I am so afraid you might not be pleased here but I say come & see, bring ma too & let her see; it will improve y'r health & then you will know for y'rself & if you don't like it you can go else where. [4 December 1881]

While Clinton scouted available land in the canyon, Anna and the children lived with the Jones family in their newly acquired home. Likewise, Maria and Laura Lynn were guests of the Jones family during December 1881. Relationships among the three families were cordial in spite of their crowded living arrangement. On Monday, 12 December, Anna wrote her mother a letter while William Jones installed a stove in the kitchen, prompting Anna to explain, "If my letter is flighty you will know the cause." The Stoner and Jones children played well together, Anna reported. While her children remained healthy during the journey and during their early weeks in the canyon,

119

Anna reported illness among the Jones children, including one who suffered chills and worms. Although she believed the child had not received the correct treatment for her malady, Anna declined saying so to Mattie Jones, viewing the matter as "none of my business." The only incident Anna recorded in which trouble arose between the two families occurred when William Jones threw one of Anna's kittens against a tent pole and killed it. Anna reported to her mother that "Clinton was ready to settle it with him," but Jones apologized and asked that they not tell his wife and Maria Lynn what he had done [12 December 1881]. In this minor event, both men revealed something of their relationships to women. Clinton, who had once apologized profusely for killing one of Anna's mother's chickens, was ready to fight with his friend when Jones killed one of Anna's kittens. Jones's repentance over the incident centered upon his anxiety concerning the disapproval his wife and sister-in-law might express about his embarrassing loss of temper. Just as the women of the Stoner and Jones families carried the tenets of nineteenth-century womanhood with them to the frontier, the men sought to maintain the image of chivalry.

While living with the Joneses, the Stoner family spent their first Christmas in the canyon, an experience quite different from their previous Christmas holidays in Victoria County, where Anna and Clinton stayed home and celebrated quietly. Their first Christmas in the canyon, in a home filled with nine eager children, was an exciting time, and Anna conveyed in a letter to her mother how much she enjoyed it. Later, when Martha responded to Anna's letter, she exclaimed that her daughter's tale "cheered me up considerably I assure you. Your description of the happy faces around the well filled stockings was so plain I could almost see them" [5 January 1882]. Anna's narrative began and ended with her children's reactions to the events in the Joneses' home on Sunday, 25 December 1881:

> Well the children had a general jubile over Sante Claus
> present[s] this morning. There were *only ten* stockens

hung up last night, from that negrow Tete down to Mrs. J's baby.(by the way that negrow is the only *jenteelman of culler* up here) Apples, dates ammonds, raisens, & fancy & stick candy & a few pretties for the bigger ones was the order of the day. Mrs. J & myself clubed together to make cakes & pies for dinner so we had a good dinner today a *better* one tomorrow & a *best* one the next day; as no one but home folks were here today, & tommorrow a genteelman & his wife & the mail rider will dine here & Tuesday the youthfull presbyterian minister from Uvalde will dine here so you see 'the big pot will be put in the little one' then & kept there, untill the Monday following when he will return again to his city or one horse town home. . . . I do wish you could have seen Hope & Royal this morning. I dressed them before it was day as the others were getting up & the[y] came to get them to take them in Mrs. J's room to see the stockens full so I let them go then slip[p]ed on my cloths as quick as possible & went in too. They wouldn't let the children touch the things untill all had seen them. When I went in Hope began to laugh & chatter & dance just as fast as her little feet could go up & down & point at the stockens & look at me all the same, and Roy? Well he just sit up there in daddies lap & smiled from ear to ear & show[ed] all three of his little teeth as if he was old Cris Crincle himself. Hope's doll that Maggie [Stoner] gave her had on a new dress so she carried the doll & stocken in one arm & hand while she eat with the other. [25 December 1881]

By the time the Stoners completed their first two months in the Nueces River canyon, they were familiar with the environment, comfortable with the housing situation, convinced of the healthfulness of the climate, and acquainted with almost the entire community. Before long, they themselves began extending hospitality to newly arriving families.

121

Everyone Here Has Lived in a Tent
January–March 1882

Anna's written portrayal of the rough, yet interesting country to which she had come intrigued her father-in-law, and on
Christmas Eve, 1881, Thomas Chilton Stoner surprised the
family, arriving, like Santa Claus, with a trunk filled with
gifts of clothing and shoes. When the excitement of the holidays diminished, Clinton's father looked over his new surroundings. In spite of the opportunities he saw there for
hunting and fishing, he reacted negatively to the canyon. In
January, Anna exclaimed to Martha, "Clinton's Pa is with us &
the most disgusted white man that I ever saw. He says this is
the last place on earth & he thinks is not fit for any thing but
Indians and Mexicans." Soon after Thomas C. Stoner's arrival,
the railroad reached Uvalde, and newcomers began pouring
into the canyon. Anna reported to Martha that families had arrived from counties all over Texas and from as far east as New
York and from as far west as California, and among the immigrants were "two green Englishmen" [n.d. January 1882]. Earlier, news of the popularity of the region reached Martha
Wellington in Victoria County, where she heard that the Mc-
Faddins planned to move a large herd of cattle into the canyon.
She wrote Anna the news and urged the Stoners to consider
carefully the wisdom of settling in the canyon when overgraz-
ing was a distinct possibility [23 December 1881]. Her mother's
doubts about the potential of making a living in the region, her
own awareness that the canyon could not support the number
of families moving in, and her father-in-law's resolute dislike
for the canyon all combined to shake Anna's confidence. In January 1882, she wrote her mother:

> I dont like this place well enough to settle & I believe
> Clinton doesnt like it hardly as well as I do so you see we
> are not attached to it. I know Brother would not live here

after he had seen it, now you need'nt to tell every body
this. I wish you were here so we could talk.

Anna's glowing accounts a month earlier of the region's high
mountains, clear streams, and friendly people, as seen through
her own eyes, dimmed in January, when she viewed the canyon
through her father-in-law's eyes. "I just tell you," she wrote
Martha, "if you will cover the whole face of the earth with low
thorn bushes that will average as high as shaperal down there
& put bare mountains and rocks all through it you will about
have it."

While winter settled in the canyon, a bright spot emerged to
lighten Anna's growing doubt. Just after Thomas C. Stoner arrived, Anna and Clinton left the Joneses' home and moved into
their own home, a tent. On the journey from Victoria County,
the Stoners used a small tent for shelter; upon arriving in the
Nueces River canyon, they discovered that many settlers lived
in larger tents because of scarcities in building materials. Anna
assured her mother that "the tents are as comfortable as
houses & some as well furnished where people live year after
year." Some of the "house-shaped tents" had chimneys and
some had stoves. When Clinton decided that he could not locate a suitable house, he ordered from San Antonio a tent,
fourteen feet by eighteen feet, for the price of twenty-six dollars. He and his father erected the tent, perhaps bought from
military surplus, on the Joneses' land near Montell Creek [n.d.
January 1882].

Around the campfire beside their tent one evening in mid-
January, Clinton and Anna discussed their future with Thomas
C. Stoner, who proposed for the young couple an alternative to
settling in the canyon he found so distasteful. When Clinton
told his father that someone had made an offer to buy his entire
sheep herd, the elder Stoner encouraged his son to accept the
offer quickly and return with him to Illinois where he would
help Clinton settle and begin a farm. Anna told Martha that
Thomas C. Stoner made the following proposal:

He said he wanted him [Clinton] & Tom to take charge of
the farm after this year & let him go to tradeing & they
rais the produce & he buy the stock to feed it to & then
divide the profit & loss, that he had enough to supply us
untill we could make a crop & that we should put our
money at interest untill a certain peace of land that is to
be sold soon would be sold & then he would help him to
buy it. We are to live with them this year & after to live in
the renters house if we want to.

Although Thomas Stoner had not mentioned his plan to Anna
and Clinton before that evening, Anna was not surprised by it.
She wrote Martha:

I told you in my last letter that Clintons Pa was much dis-
satisfied with this country & that I believe he wanted us
to go home with him to live. I thought so by his telling the
children that 'granpa was going to take them home with
him when he went' & granpa want lieve his babies down
here to get killed or 'raised up here in this brush,' & all
such things as that every once in a while when he had
been playing with the children would be his winding up
speech.

The day after Stoner made the offer, Clinton and Anna pon-
dered the pros and cons of moving to Illinois, the outcome of
which Anna described to her mother: "Clinton and I had a talk
about it, I didn't say I'd go, so Clinton said he wouldn't go unless I was satisfied to go." For Anna, the major obstacle to the
move was leaving her mother and brother, and Clinton suggested that Anna write her mother to invite her to join them in
Illinois:

I thought I would write to you about it & see what you
would say to going too if Brother (bless his dear soul)
would be willing to it, if it would suit his business arraing-
ments—of course we would'nt go untill spring & it would
only cost your boarding expinces which would'nt be much.

124

Anna assured her mother that Clinton promised "he would be a son to you if you wanted to go and would do all for you that he could." Hoping to keep Thomas Stoner's offer confidential, Anna wrote across the front of her letter, in large letters, "Don't tell this to anyone but Brother please" [16 January 1882].

As the Stoners considered their future, they continued the daily tasks of providing food, shelter, and clothing for their family. Anna's goal remained the same as always even in a primitive camp environment along a rushing creek: she was determined to remain a lady, wearing the same cumbersome dresses worn earlier on the farm, attempting to cook the same meals over a campfire as formerly in a wood stove, providing the same moral instruction for her children that she had received from Bible study and school in her youth, and doing all without complaint and under submission to her husband. Clinton's mother, Nancy Hathaway Stoner, suggested, however, that under living conditions as unsettled as Anna's, a woman's role changed and she deserved more help from her husband. In late January, after Thomas Chilton Stoner had been in Texas for a month without writing his wife and children in Illinois, her mother-in-law sent Anna the following advice:

> I now fully realize my own situation & yours too, Pa is so carried away with Texas fishing he does not stop even to think of us much less write us a letter he is off by the break of day gathering in the trout if Clinton is not with him, his sheep & horses command his attention while you are at home with the little ones brooding over trials of the day, writing to me, & planning over something for their dinner on their return . . . [Then] you are up all in a hury to . . . relieve them of their cares—which has been only play for them (if they have been fishing) dont do it—let them get the fish & let them dress them, while you have the skillet hot to cook them after they get them ready &

your part is done, if you attend to your little children do your washing & ironing do your cooking then live in a tent your hands are full, if you haven't water at the door never let them leave you at any time without getting you plenty of water right at the tent door & everything else that man can do to relieve womans lot, *in your situation* if they dont offer, ask them to do it for man most always would do these things if we will ask them if they don't think of it without. [21 January 1882]

In the meantime, Thomas Wellington arrived in the canyon to visit the Stoners and see for himself how his sister fared. His impression of the area echoed that of Thomas C. Stoner. The canyon was suitable for neither cattle nor sheep, Thomas reported to Martha, but "for goats Rattle snakes and rabbits, it is the finest place I ever saw in my life." He questioned the honesty of settlers who claimed to love the overstocked canyon, writing, "Some people here pretend to think that this is a heaven on earth but they will all offer to *sell* at one dollar or rent their land at two cents per acre." As for the Stoner family's living arrangements, Thomas Wellington told Martha that the tent lacked privacy and leaked when it rained. Furthermore, he had not found Anna in as good health as her letters purported, but she suffered painful headaches. He also verified the attempts of Thomas C. Stoner to persuade Clinton to return to Illinois [6 February 1882].

Thomas's negative reaction to the canyon, plus his reports of Anna's illness and the possibility of her moving out of Texas, heightened Martha's anxieties about the Stoner's safety and comfort. Knowing how her mother would react to Thomas's February letter, Anna attempted to lessen Martha's worries in her next letter. To dispel her mother's concerns about her family's living arrangements, Anna wrote an extensive description of the interior of her tent-house, allowing a rare, first-hand account of a nineteenth-century settler's home. First, she explained that since living in the tent, they had experienced two or three hard rains, and only one "misted" through the tent, and that was the rain that occurred during Thomas's visit. Anna assured her mother that she and Clinton devised ways to keep the family dry:

> Do not be troubled about us sleeping in the rain for as soon as the tent was set (which by the way is a *large* one) Clinton drove forks in the ground and laid two stout poles across the ends & then laid poles length-wise of the bed close together so we could put on the beds & they would not sink through in places as they do on bed slats, & it makes very comfortable beds, no high or higher than the bed I had in the front room; I have so many things next to the poles & the feather beds on top of them that they are not only high & dry but very comfortable too. . . . I'd much rather be in the tent than some of the houses that some of these people live in. I sprinkle the floor every once in a while to keep the dust laid but in an hour after it is wet it is dry again so you see we are not troubled with wet or even damp ground inside of the tent.

Then, Anna's letter carried her mother on a visual tour of her family's new home, where barrels and boxes became useful furniture:

> I have two beds up with the heads to the back of the tent & my [sewing] machine sitting between them right against the tent pole . . . at the foot of one bed there is two trunks & then comes the *'pantry'* a barrel of floor meal, barrel [of] salt, and another barrel with harness & such things in it; on the other side I have a trunk at the foot of the bed & in the front corner of the tent opposite the 'pantry' is the 'beauro' a large dry goods box set on end & covered with paper on top and a curtain in front; in that I put some clean clothes & keep my dirty clothes in it;

> on top is my lamp and combs etc. etc. In the middle of the
> front of the tent I have a box for a table & in it I keep the
> oil can, coffee & other things. Under one of the beds is
> other boxes with sugar, rice etc. in them, so you see I
> have plenty of room & am as comfortable on a cold or wet
> day as most of my neighbors.

The pleasant picture painted for Martha Wellington contained the subtle message that while her new house was not like her former one in Victoria County, Anna felt all right about where she lived. It was as good a home as her neighbors had, so she did not feel separated socially from them. Clinton had not neglected the family's needs for dry shelter or privacy in setting up the tent. In hopes that Martha would decide to visit the canyon soon, Anna assured her of privacy: "We will have our bedroom curtained off to ourselves. I'll show you how comfortable we can be in a tent." Anna also sought to reassure her mother of the family's health and contentment. Upon hearing from Thomas about Anna's headaches, Martha Wellington sent her daughter violets to relieve her symptoms. Anna addressed her mother's anxiety in her letter:

> Now about my neuralgia. I have not had it since brother
> left & I believe it was caused from my courses stopping
> but they came all right on the fourth of this month while
> Brother was here so you see I was at my sickest while he
> was here. I think it was cold stop[p]ed them for I had no
> simtoms of pregnancy or a miscarriage & since I was un-
> well I have been perfectly well all of the time & am very
> much stronger than I ever was before I came up here but I
> am very thankful to get the violets. I shall keep them in
> case of neccesity & will most ashuredly use them if I ever
> have it again.

Next, Anna disclosed more about the nature of her father-in-law's offer to Clinton concerning a move to Illinois, an offer

Anna considered generous. Stoner would give his son fifty-two acres, along with teams and implements to farm the land, for a share of ten bushels of corn per acre. Stoner's proposal appealed to Anna, but she confided feelings of ambiguity to her mother:

> I know I could always get along with his Pa & believe I
> could with the others, too. . . . Clinton is no stock man—
> farming is his trade. . . . I think we would have more com-
> forts there than here & I want to go & yet I do not know
> whether to decide to go or not. [23 February 1882]

Before she received Anna's letter, Martha Wellington decided to visit the canyon herself to help hasten the Stoners' decision. On the same day that her son returned from his trip to Uvalde County, Martha wrote Anna that she planned to reach San Antonio by "private conveyance" and board a train for Uvalde, where she hoped Clinton would meet her. By now the overwrought mother was so concerned about her daughter and grandchildren that she was willing to go with them anywhere they chose, whether in the canyon or elsewhere:

> Tho's saw no place, while returning that he liked any bet-
> ter than the place Clinton went to see near Capt. Clubbs—
> I hope C. like it better up there than the place he is at &
> will be able to decide where he will settle by the time I
> get there, even If it should be in Ill. I would even be will-
> ing to go with you there If you so decide but it is entirely
> too early to go North yet & I would have to return to Tex.
> in the Fall, as I could not stand it in that cold climate. [27
> February 1882][22]

Martha Wellington postponed her trip to Uvalde one month, and during that time, her children reached their own decisions about their futures and, consequently, hers.

The Stoners' uncertainty in late February gave way to a decisive outcome by early March. Writing hastily in order to take the letter to the Joneses' before the mail rider left, Anna explained to her mother that Clinton had left for an extended visit to Bandera and Concho counties to look for land. He decided "he is going to find him a place in Texas if it is possible, that he does not want to go north if he can get a foot hold in the South any where" [5 March 1882]. Clinton and Anna chose to remain in South Texas and make their home in its western fringes. Not as impressed as Thomas Wellington with the land above Captain Clubb's place, high in the hills along Montell Creek, Clinton eliminated that site from consideration. Anna explained for Martha his reasoning, which pleased her:

> He says he does not see where we could live up there & that we women folks could never see any one that was worth seeing but men unless we were put in the waggon & hauled down in the cannion over the worst kind of a rocky rode.

Anna's former sense of well-being returned once Clinton had taken decisive action. Each letter received from Victoria County mentioned sickness among their former neighbors and friends there. In contrast, Anna boasted to Martha from her home in the mountain canyon, "The children are growing bigger, stronger & it seems healthier & I know *browner* every day so am I getting strong & brown" [5 March 1882].

Upon hearing the Stoners' decision to stay in South Texas, Martha Wellington wrote Anna that she had completed her plans to visit them. Thomas busied himself gathering yearlings to move to pasture he had located in Frio County on his return trip from the hill country to the coastal plain, and Martha prepared to accompany him on the drive. Once the cattle reached their destination, Thomas planned to take Martha to visit Anna while he searched for a place in which he and his mother could settle. Martha and Thomas were not alone in leaving Victoria County in early 1882. The Garnett family left for Bandera, Martha wrote Anna, adding, "many of our neighbors are anxious to leave here for the sake of health for their families—the River's overflows are on the increase & consequently the sickness too." Clinton's father would return to Illinois soon, and Martha Wellington confessed to Anna her relief that she and her daughter would not be following him:

> I hope he will not leave the state with disgust but will eventually make this country his future home—I believe it would add many years to his life by moving to a warm climate— I am perfectly *sincere* in what I say, for you know, I have had some experience on that subject, in your *Papa's case*, for I am sure he could not have lived as long as he did *here*, if he had remained in that cold country and that was the cause of his coming to Texas—'For what is life, without health.' [27 March 1882]

* * * * *

Anna's ambivalence about leaving Texas, where her mother and brother wanted to stay, probably influenced Clinton's decision against returning to Illinois, and perhaps his father's visit reminded Clinton of the reasons he left home initially. Clinton Stoner could find independence and self-sufficiency only by distancing himself from his father's overbearing influence. On the frontier, as their choices became more independent, Anna and Clinton Stoners' marriage became more complex and relational than formerly in Victoria County. Clinton accepted Anna's need for female companionship and kinship ties, factors he intended to consider in making a choice of where they would settle. Overcrowding of stock and unavailability of houses in the lower Nueces River canyon, combined with his initial success in keeping sheep, spurred his interest in lands farther north on the Edwards Plateau. In March 1882, while his father stayed with Anna, Hope, and Thomas Royal, Clinton traveled by horseback northward up the Nueces River canyon in search of land. While he was gone, Anna began to realize how much his companionship had come to mean to her. Her father-in-law assumed the role of family protector and provider, chopping wood, hauling water, building fires, hunting game, fishing, and playing with the children. Beyond that, though, Anna recognized that Clinton had become her confidant. She wrote her mother: "I do hope he will find one [a place to live] for I never want him to have to go so far away again, not that I need any thing or that he could help me any more than his pa does, but still I miss him" [5 March 1882]. The Stoners' experience on the journey to the lower Nueces River canyon and during their search for a new home solidified their partnership while preparing them individually for difficult times ahead.

4
Grace to Conquer

Edwards County
April 1882–March 1884

Cattle raisers and farmers scrutinizing the economic potential of the Edwards Plateau of Texas in the early 1880s soon discovered the truth of a statement written about the region in the 1867 *Texas Almanac:* "Very few, if any, have had the temerity to try to live there."[1] First surveyed in 1859 by Charles de Montel, Edwards County, on the southern Edwards Plateau, remained unorganized until 1883. Renegade Indians menaced the area until 1882, and lack of rail transportation further inhibited development. The nearest rail station was in Uvalde, a full day's ride south by horseback from the Edwards–Uvalde county line. Not until 1876 did the first permanent settler buy

133

a block of state school land in the county and build the first lumber house in the area from materials hauled across Texas from Nacogdoches. In the first federal census of Edwards County, compiled in 1880, only 266 inhabitants lived in the county's nearly one thousand square miles. Of the forty-nine heads of households recorded, almost one half professed to be farmers, the other half, stock raisers. In addition, the county census listed one merchant, two blacksmiths, one mail carrier, one seamstress, one goatherder (the only non-white resident in the county), one retired professor of science, and two men whose occupation was "doing nothing." Only 140 qualified voters lived in the county on 10 April 1883, when Edwards County became officially organized, with the town of Leakey as county seat.[2]

Attracted by favorable grazing lands, stock raisers entered Edwards County in the early 1880s seeking ranch sites along the narrow, fertile valleys created by the east and middle forks of the Nueces River, the west fork of the Frio River, the south Llano River, and the waters of Cedar, Hackberry, and Bull Head creeks. The black limestone soil near the rivers and creeks was deep enough to support small vegetable gardens, and irrigation ditches dug from springs and streams furnished sufficient moisture for small-scale farming. The soil on the county's southern hills and northern prairies was too shallow, arid, and rocky to foster the development of large-scale farming, but the land sustained forage grasses and brush particularly well suited for goats. As in neighboring Uvalde County, native pecan trees flourished along the river bottoms and beehives filled caves in the area, providing settlers with two natural sources of income: pecans and honey.

The canyon cut by the meandering east prong of the Nueces River extended southward more than forty miles from northeastern Edwards County into Uvalde County. At Camp Wood, ten miles north of the Montell community in Uvalde County, a Texas Rangers station protected scattered canyon settlements from fugitive Indian bands and white outlaws who frequently hid among the area's hills, caves, and canyons. Four miles north of Camp Wood was the community of Dixie, later called Barksdale, where a hotel, saloon, and store developed. About six miles farther north in the canyon, where Bull Head Creek rushed into the Nueces River from the east, was a store and post office also called Bull Head, which served as the county seat of Edwards County prior to its organization in 1883.[3] About ten miles farther upstream, the settlement of Hackberry formed near the confluence of Hackberry Creek and the Nueces River.

In March 1882, when Clinton Stoner left his wife and children in the care of his father in a tent beside Montell Creek, his original intention was to investigate land throughout the Edwards Plateau, from Bandera to Concho counties. However, only twenty-eight miles north of his family's camp site, he located recently vacated land with improvements. No evidence exists to indicate why the former owners left the property in Edwards County, but families moved in and out of the Nueces River canyon with little notice during those early days of settlement in the region. The improvements on the land included a log house, springhouse, and smokehouse and so attracted Clinton that he overlooked his earlier promise to find a place where Anna could easily visit other women. No deed record exists concerning the Stoners' purchase of the land, but before the end of March 1882, the Stoner family relocated to their new home in the upper Nueces River canyon, eight miles above Bull Head and two miles below Hackberry.[4]

In the first year in their dirt-floored log home among the hills of the upper Nueces River canyon, Clinton and Anna Stoner maintained as much contact with their extended family as possible. In fact, one or more of their relatives lived with the Stoners every month but three from March 1882 to March 1883. Thomas Chilton Stoner helped move Clinton and Anna into their home in Edwards County in late March 1882 before

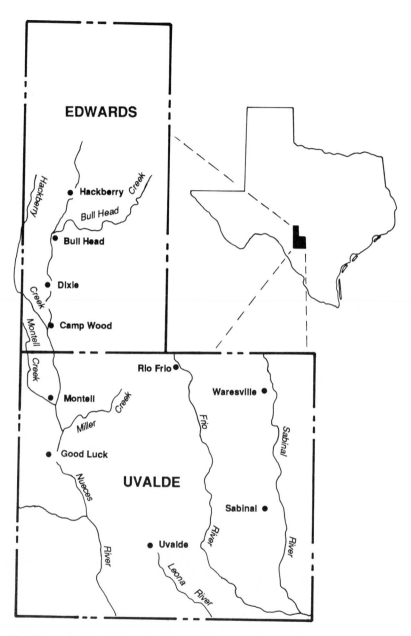

Uvalde and Edwards Counties, Texas, 1884.

he returned to Illinois. Martha Wellington resided with the Stoners from mid-April to September 1882, during which time Thomas Wellington, seeking a cure for his diabetic condition, visited various doctors in Goliad and San Antonio. Anna wrote Thomas at least three times during those five months, and Martha wrote her son twice. Several of Anna's letters mentioned in her mother's and brother's replies have not survived to the present. From September 1882 to March 1883, Anna wrote Thomas and Martha, who had just settled in San Antonio, at least five times each. During that period, Thomas sent Anna four letters and one postcard, and Martha wrote her daughter four letters. In December 1882, Thomas C. Stoner returned to the canyon with his wife and young daughters, and they remained with Anna and Clinton through March 1883. Clinton's father tried again to persuade his son to move back to Illinois or join him in another location in West Texas. Anna's mother and brother advised her to move near their new home in Bexar County. When they realized that the couple was content in the Nueces River canyon and not inclined to move, both sides of the family considered relocating their own homes to the canyon area. Financial hardship visited both the Thomas C. Stoners and the Wellingtons during 1882, and they looked to their children for help.

The heading of Anna's first letter from Edwards County, written on 1 April 1882, indicates that she once again felt "at home," an expression used in her letters written in Victoria County. She continued to describe her new environment as she did in her letters from Uvalde County, but now used fewer metaphors. Her language revealed a growing familiarity with her surroundings and a developing sense of confidence about handling the demands of frontier life. The Stoners visited other newcomers in the area and received occasional news about former Victoria County friends, but their social contacts in the upper canyon were less frequent than before in the more populated lower canyon. Anna's letters contained more news about crops and stock than news about homemaking and local society, perhaps because her visitors in the Bull Head region were more often male than female and more of her letters from the upper Nueces River canyon were addressed to her brother than her mother. Her letters contained practical advice and poignant encouragements to boost Thomas's declining hopes for overcoming his illness. Anna's 1882–1883 Edwards County letters disclose information about early families living within the upper Nueces River canyon that is unavailable from public documents. Court records, including deed transactions, tax lists, and probate records for Edwards County during the period in which the Stoners lived there are nonexistent. The county remained unorganized until 1883, and a courthouse fire destroyed what few records existed prior to 1884. Although community life interested Anna, family life was primary to her. Her letters from the Bull Head post office focused on her immediate family's environment and daily life and upon her extended family's financial and health problems. Maintaining ties with family members through personal letters continued to provide a sense of continuity for the Stoners between their isolated world and the larger community.

A Real Mountain Home
April–September 1882

Clinton and Anna Stoner moved into the upper Nueces River canyon in late March 1882 onto land already partially developed. In addition to the log home, springhouse, and smokehouse, the previous owners left behind livestock pens and a horse shed, as well as a garden in full bloom and a number of chickens. In her first letter to her mother after her family's move to Edwards County, Anna characterized her new location, situated among hills that rose to elevations of 2,000 to

2,500 feet, as "a real 'mountain' home." The upper canyon, she
wrote, "is much narrower here than it is down about Montell
and is rougher of course." Her reactions to the lower canyon
had been ambivalent; she had both liked and disliked the rugged valleys and swift running streams and river. From the upper canyon, however, Anna wrote her mother: "I am very
much pleased with this place so far and think it can be made a
beautifull and plessent home." Only six years had passed since
the first family settled in the upper Nueces Canyon, and the
informal atmosphere of the frontier prevailed when the Stoners
arrived. As in the lower canyon, many families in the area still
lived in tents. Anna warned her mother, "You must expect to
see the roughest kind of a house when you get here. The room
I use for a kitchen has no floor in it & the house is log hewed
on the inside & the cracks are boarded up with clapboards, and
this is one of the *finest* houses in this part of the cannion."

The Stoner's new ranch utilized the natural terrain and water resources to the best advantage, a fact Anna explained to
her mother in the following way:

> The river Neuesses runs close by the yard fence just un-
> der the hill there, you know, & is about half as big as it
> was where we camped. Brother can tell you how wide that
> was, the principal part of it here comes out of our field as
> the largest spring I have ever seen rises in the middle of it
> & runs along the side of my garden, the garden can be
> irigated from it.

With abundant spring water, the garden prospered, and Anna
boasted, "There are more shalots & onions in the garden than I
ever saw in one garden before & plenty of raddishes and lettuce
to eat, lots of cabbage plants, beet plants & some tomatoe
plants too." Also, in addition to a garden, Anna once again had
chickens. "The hens are laying fine now," she wrote, "if they
will just keep it up, I set one today the only one there was
setting."

As before, the Stoners found more settled families willing to share skills and knowledge learned from their experiences in the canyon. Some neighbors, such as the Ammon Billings family, shared far more than just advice. Billings, who lived two miles north of the Stoners near the settlement of Hackberry, allowed Anna and Clinton to milk his range cows.[5] The wild, lean, Mexican cattle were poor milk producers and had to be roped and tied before they could be milked.[6] Nonetheless, Anna persisted in her efforts to milk them: "We milk 13 & get two water buckets full of milk & a gallon over, twice a day, & give the calves half. We just milk two tits, so you see we have all the milk & butter we can use & more too." Having resumed many of the chores she did on her Victoria County farm, Anna discovered her children, one now almost three years old and the other a sixteen-month-old toddler, distracted her from her tasks. She told her mother, "Hope & Royal (Royal esspescially) have bothered me untill I cant get things straight; I was churning just before I commenced this letter & they had to help, so now they think they must help write too."

In her April first letter, Anna laid out the plans devised for Martha's visit to the canyon. Clinton intended to bring his father to Uvalde in mid-April to catch the train for the first leg of his return trip to Illinois, and, because Clinton would not return to Uvalde until the next fall, he asked Martha to meet him there at that time so that he could bring her in the wagon to Edwards County. Anna prepared Martha for a long trip from the train station:

> It is 65 miles from here to Uvalde & over a very rough rocky road it will take two days to make the trip the night you are out you will stay at some of the houses down in the Montell neighborhood just which ever the horses can get too that night. If nothing happens to any of us I know you will all meet there on the 16th. . . . if you get there before Clinton does enquiere for W. F. Burketts & I'll

write to him to see that you get comfortable board while
you are there. He is the P. M. [postmaster] & the man we
deal with down there & is a nice man. Clinton and his Pa
will start from here today two weeks (today is saturday &
I suppose the first of Apr) that would make it the 15 that
they lieve here, Sunday night they will get to Uvalde so
that Pa can take the train Monday morning or the 17th,
that is the programe so far.

She also suggested that Martha not wait until arriving in
Uvalde to buy any supplies she wanted to bring to the canyon,
but rather make her purchases in San Antonio, where prices
were lower. Then, she requested specifically, "When you come
through San Antonio pleas get me as cheap a striking clock as
you can & I'll pay you for it *if it will not make you lose too
much time* & get Hope a doll, but *I will not pay you for that,
may be*, so there!" [1 April 1882].

In mid-April 1882, at the new Uvalde train depot, Clinton
bade his father farewell and greeted his mother-in-law. After
staying one night with William and Mattie Jones on Montell
Creek, Clinton and Martha arrived at the Stoners' mountain
home on the eighteenth of April. Three days later, Martha
wrote her son Thomas about her trip and her first impressions
of the canyon: "I arrived safe at Clints home in the mountains
on the 18th inst *very* tired, but well and found all well. . . .
From what I have seen of the Canion I like it much better than
I expected though I do not think I would *prefer* this out-of-
the-way place for a home." Martha confided to her son that
Thomas C. Stoner left the area with the intention of returning
in the fall with his wife and youngest children so that they
could help him determine whether or not to leave Illinois and
move to Texas while land was still inexpensive. "But," Martha
added, "he does not think of locating up here but want Clint to
sell out & go with him to a better farming country if it is to be
found in western Tex." Upon seeing Anna's new home in

Edwards County, Martha received much sought-after reassurance concerning her daughter's welfare. During Clinton's absence in Uvalde, Maria Stoner Lynn came up from Montell to stay with Anna and the children and spent her time there fishing, "so," Martha told Thomas, "I have a nice mess of fish for dinner today." Also, the fact that the families of the Hackberry community had built a new schoolhouse, which served ten to twelve students, bolstered Martha's opinion of the settlers in the canyon. Martha made no complaint about Anna's rough living conditions, and bragged about Clinton's accomplishments:

> Clint's crop is very good near the house and we have vegetables on the table every day, but I have not seen his field yet as it is some distance from the house. He can irrigate his corn & garden with all ease as it lies between two springs & he has a ditch already prepared for it. [21 April 1882]

The daily life of the Stoner family through the spring and summer months of 1882 revolved around the outdoor work of maintaining and protecting their stock and garden, procuring supplemental food through fishing and hunting, and improving their house and out buildings. Anna assumed the roles she played previously in Victoria County: maintaining the garden and poultry, milking and churning, preparing meals and doing laundry, and caring for the children. Poor roads and long distances between ranches prevented Anna from traveling alone to visit other area women, but when newcomers arrived, she and Clinton rode together to greet them. Clinton kept his fields and livestock, hunted game, made weekly shopping and mail trips to Bull Head and semi-annual trading trips to Uvalde, and did necessary carpentry work on their buildings. Martha shared chores with Anna and played with Hope and Royal. Both Martha and Anna kept in contact with Thomas Wellington through frequent letters and postcards, some of which have not survived. At the end of May, Anna wrote Thomas that

Clinton had five hundred head of goats. He himself herded them for a week or two, Anna reported, then hired a herder; once trained, the goats no longer required a herder. During daylight, the goats roamed freely among the brush on the hilly canyon slopes above the house, and at twilight, they returned on their own to pens, which provided protection from predators. Anna also reported to Thomas that her daily efforts at milking resulted in about three pounds of butter each day. She packed the butter in buckets in the springhouse, where, she claimed, it stayed hard because "the water is almost cold enough to make your teeth ache" [28 May 1882]. Having more butter than the family needed, Clinton sometimes bartered the extra pounds in Bull Head.

The Bull Head store served as a gathering place and post office for scattered settlers in the upper Nueces River canyon. Neighbors passing the Stoners' ranch on their way to Bull Head frequently stopped to visit, offering to return with supplies and mail for the family. Canyon storekeepers hauled provisions from Uvalde or Kerrville at great cost, and supplies usually failed to meet local demand. Anna reported that the Bull Head store ran out of salt once when she needed it and out of quinine another time. Occasionally, peddlers traveled through the canyon with wagonloads of household goods, and from one of them Anna bought a set of chairs. The Bull Head store provided many of the Stoners' year-round supplies, but twice a year Clinton traveled the sixty-five miles south to Uvalde to trade at the store of W. F. Burkett. Besides keeping a store, Burkett was the Stoner's banker, holding a certain amount of their cash in an account on which they could write notes.

On 10 July Anna wrote Thomas about two large social events among canyon settlers, a double wedding and an Independence Day celebration. Martha declined attending either occasion because, Anna explained, "the rode was so rocky," choosing instead to stay with Hope and Royal while Clinton and Anna went. "I hated very much to leive her here," Anna wrote, "but she declared she was not afraid and did'nt mind it and would rather stay than to go and that she wanted me to go so that was the way of it." The double wedding took place in June seven miles down the Nueces River at the Woodruff ranch, where brides named Woodruff and Webber married brothers named Baker. According to Anna's letter, about two hundred people gathered for the barbecue following the private wedding ceremony. Anna and Clinton did not stay for the dance that followed the barbecue, but Anna heard later that "the young people 'triped their light fantastic toes' untill daylight and many of them . . . took breakfast there." The following week, Mr. Webber, father of one of the brides, hosted another party, or "infare," for the couples, but the Stoners did not attend. Newlywed couples, such as the Bakers, lived in tents in the canyon until they could afford to haul in lumber to build a house.

A few weeks after the wedding, Anna and Clinton again rode horseback down the canyon to Bull Head, where the community celebrated the Fourth of July with another barbecue and dance. There Anna met many of the women from the canyon who, like her, seldom left their homes. Again, the Stoners did not stay for the dance, but Anna reported to her brother that the "ball" had taken place in a store still in the process of being built. She wrote, "It had no roof on it but had a good floor and the wall up, so they danced under the stars I suppose." At the July Fourth celebration in Bull Head, Anna discovered a woman she had previously known in Victoria County. The woman, whose family had preceded the Stoners in settling in Edwards County, was "old Mrs. Sanches," Anna reported to Thomas. She described their meeting to her brother in the following narrative, in which Anna tried to imitate the older woman's dialect:

> This is the way it was, I was talking to a lady & an old
> bent woman came along an stoped on the other side of her

144

& kept looking at me, I thought she did'nt know any better so i did'nt notice it, very soon she stooped down &
whispered something to the lady I had been talking to & I
heard her answer that 'that was her name' I did'nt know
that she was talking about me, but the old woman raised
up & said, 'is you Ma liven yet Miss Stoner" I said 'yes-
mam' then she said, 'why is she now?' I told her, she said
'I'de like ter see her' 'I aint seen her in a long time, I use
ter liv close ter where you lived my chillun an you wernt
to school togeder to Miss Ann Huff when we use ter keep
Cummels ferry thar thar's is My Button now, dont you see
him? an Winny she's married an a liven over here on
Pulliam. So there is where it started & ended, they call
themselves Indian instead of Mex.

Since Royal W. Wellington's death in 1875 and Anna's marriage in 1877, Thomas Wellington had tried various occupations
to earn a comfortable living for his mother. During the spring
of 1882, while his mother visited Anna, Thomas considered either ranching in Frio County or dairying in San Antonio.
Throughout the following summer, while experimenting with
various cures to ease Thomas's diabetic attacks, doctors in Goliad and San Antonio advised him his illness was incurable. As-
serting the doctors were wrong, Anna wrote, "And Brother,
dont give up or get low spirited & make up your mind that you
will get well whether or not and let your whole attention be to
that point, dont let any doctor make you believe that your disease is incureable I dont believe in that and you must not either." Anna believed that positive thought would help Thomas
recuperate:

Ma says keep up a good heart & not give up if the Dr.
does & trust in Providence & you will come out all right,
& that is just what I think too. Do not be discouraged that
is half the battle you know the hymn says 'Oh do not be
discouraged for Jesus is your friend. He will give you
grace to conquer & will keep you to the end.'

145

Besides encouraging Thomas to think positively, Anna recommended certain practical ways to restore his health, including dietary changes. He reported to Anna in an earlier, now lost, letter that he had plenty of figs and fish to eat there in the house near Anaqua in Victoria County. For preserving the figs, Anna suggested two procedures:

> If you will gather your figs when they are ripe and not break all of the stems off then put ½ lb. of brown or white sugar to 1 lb. of figs and enough water to cover them well, then let them boill untill they are done well, then take out the figs and continue to boil your syrup untill it is thick then put in your figs again, let them come to a boil once more and bottle them while they are hot, I think you will have some nice preserves. You can dry them by spreading them out in the sun every day and takeing them in at night untill they are dry and then pack in a box they will keep with or without a layer of sugar between them they should be examined occasionally if the sugar is added to them.

For Thomas's fish, Anna suggested he not fry them all the time, but "roast some before the fire as you would beef ribs and stew some of it by a variety of ways of cooking it you will not tire of it so soon" [10 July 1882].

Nine days after Anna wrote Thomas, Martha also wrote him. She and Anna received two letters and a card, no longer extant, from Thomas, informing them that he was gaining strength. In spite of his improvement, Martha warned her son emphatically, "Do not go to work *too soon & cause a relapse, Hire hands* to *help* you & make *them do the hard work* & try not to ride *too much* or *very hard* in gathering the stock." When he felt well, Thomas rounded up cattle and horses to sell to raise money so that he and Martha could resettle outside of Victoria County. Martha invested Thomas with power of attorney to sell her own cattle, also, and urged her son to bargain for a price that would "cover all the expenses of moving them & making us a home to live at if it *has to be* an *humble* one so there will be *no more borrowing* of *money.*" Details about the debt the Wellingtons incurred in Victoria County are missing from their correspondence, but their attempts to repay the debt became a constant concern for both mother and son. Martha knew that Thomas could raise a higher price for their stock among buyers outside of the lowlands, and suggested that he not be "*partial* nor *commit* yourself to *any one* in particular but make those moneyed men *pay* for them if they get them." Having spoken strongly about business matters, Martha backed off somewhat, and told her son

> But you must use your own judgement with regard to this business—do the best you can, for *my* suggestion is only made to caution you—Nothing could give me greater pleasure than to be with you at a home of our own & have things around us that we can take an interest in, *except, to hear* of your *improvement* in *health.*

Families continued to enter the upper Nueces River canyon, even as earlier settlers moved out. Martha reported to Thomas, "The old setlers up here are leaving & new ones coming in, *generally* of a *better class* I believe but mostly of little property." Among the newcomers were a family named Jones, who bought property near the Stoners from the Henderson family. Clinton bought "two little patches of early corn" from the Hendersons before they left the canyon, Martha told Thomas, and, while she wrote, Anna and Clinton had gone to visit the Joneses. Some families familiar to the Wellingtons and Stoners from the South Texas coast also settled temporarily in the canyon region, including cattleman Charlie McFaddin, who married Mary Ellis, whom Anna first met at the July Fourth barbecue. Other settlers known to the Wellingtons were Tom Lyman, who moved to the headwaters of the Nueces about ten miles above the Stoners, and the Jack Coward family, who preceded the Stoners into the canyon but moved elsewhere in the summer of 1882. Other families known by the Wellingtons also left Victoria County during 1882 and located homes west of San Antonio. The Garnetts and Millers moved to Bandera, Martha recalled to Thomas.

Conditions in the canyon had so improved for Anna and Clinton by mid-summer 1882 that Martha boasted to Thomas:

> A *stranger* visiting this place would think Clint was an old setler from the looks of things about here. The cows he milks, his goats, hogs, sheep & chickens are all the gentlest I ever saw & he has three stands of bees, two of them two story high. He took off the upper story of one of them filled full of the nicest honey I ever saw & with what he got out of one of his bee caves, filled a five Gal. keg full & put it in the Spring house for safe keeping.

Clinton intended to sell the honey to his cousins back in Victoria County.

Martha also reported to Thomas that Clinton had repeated his initial success with sheep with his first goat herd. "So far he says he likes the goat business better than any other stock he has ever had," she wrote, "& they are the least trouble. He doese not heard them now & they come home regular before night." The family had no fruit during the first half of summer because Clinton planted his melons too late, but his corn prospered. He told Martha that, together with the corn harvested from the Hendersons' former fields, he thought he would make two hundred bushels that summer. For her own part, Martha spent part of each day in the canyon teaching her grandchildren in the same way she had taught her own children, and she boasted of success to Thomas:

> Hope is learning to talk very plain and can count five and almost repeat the little prayer 'Now I lay me down to sleep" . . . Royal is learning to talk too, and is the stron-

gest, most active, and healthy child I ever saw of his age—They both go with Papa to pen the goats at night but are afraid of the sheep, for one of them butts. [19 July 1882]

Hope and Royal were their parents' constant companions, and although they sometimes bothered Anna with their attempts to help churn and write letters, they learned very early in life that everyone on the ranch worked.

The next extant letter from the canyon to Thomas came from Anna, who wrote in early August. Thomas was then in San Antonio, taking "Dr. Warker's Diabetes Cure." Martha was ready to join Thomas in San Antonio, so she would soon travel to Uvalde to catch the train east, and Anna hoped that she and her children could accompany her mother to the depot. Writing late in the evening after the rest of the family was asleep, Anna confided to Thomas that all was not well with their crops and garden. A heavy summer rain left their corn musty in the fields, and then "petty thieves" cut open their watermelons, planted among the corn, leaving them exposed and rotting [3 August 1882]. Once again, conditions beyond their control threatened the Stoners' annual cash crop.

Good People Moving In
September–December 1882

In September 1882, Martha Wellington left the upper Nueces River canyon. She traveled in the company of the Lyman family, and Anna and her children did not make the anticipated trip to Uvalde. Martha's narrative about her journey from the hill country to Uvalde to San Antonio constituted most of the eight-page letter she wrote to Anna two weeks after reaching her destination. The first leg of the trip went pleasantly, and she wrote Anna, "I suppose Mr. and Mrs.

149

Lyman told you of our trip to U. (& you will please give them our united thanks for their kind attention to me on the road)." In Uvalde, Martha visited the W. F. Burkett store, where she filled a trunk with twelve rolls of cotton batting and enough cotton thread for Anna to make a quilt. She sent the trunk, along with clothes and candy for the children, with the Lymans on their return to the canyon. Martha stayed overnight in Uvalde before boarding a coach the next morning for the two-mile trip to the train depot north of town. Every aspect of her trip seemed like an adventure to Martha, who described carefully for Anna her experience as a woman traveling alone:

> I had a nice room at the Hotel & a nice room mate, a young lady from D'hanis as they call it. She was a Miss Ney pronounced Naze, a descendant of Marshal Ney one of Napolian Bonaparts Marshals. Next morning the *Bus.* came around at ½ past ten full of well dressed men (two of color) three went into a Saloon near by & the coloured gents stood respectfully outside the door while I entered & found a seat. Mr. Bowls carried my satchel & helped me in. Of course, I spoke to no one, but when we reached the Depot I paid 5. cts & a gentleman steped up & offered to take my satchel & show me the way to the ladies waiting room which was emty, as there was no other lady from U. & he also got me a seat on the cars. One of the coloured gents helped the driver to carry my trunk for which I got a check, bought a ticket for 2.50 cts & waited O *so long* for the cars to come. The fare has been reduced nearly one half since last Spring.

Thomas planned to meet his mother at the Uvalde depot to accompany her back to the Alamo City, but their carefully made plans encountered complications, which Martha described for her daughter:

> Of course I reached U. one day sooner than we intended when you wrote your bro. & he promised to be there the

150

same day. I received a letter from him at B.H.P.O. [Bull Head post office] hastening my return & was glad I started so soon until I found I could not reach U. before Tues. night. Then I was fearful of passing him the next day on the Western bound Train. But I learned from Mr. Bowls, the Proprietor, that the two Trains dined at Sabinal. So I determined to risk it & when the Conductor came for my Ticket I made known my fears to him & gave him Thos' name & requested him to find him if possible. He promised & as our Train was behind time he was just in time to get *him* off, while his Train was slowly moving out. I started to the back platform & met the Conductor returning. He said, 'I have *found your boy.*' 'You *have.* Where is he?' 'On the Train, he will be here in a minute.' '*Oh, I am so glad!*' I then steped out on the platform & soon saw him coming. He stopped & looked back but soon saw me & came along as fast as he could. After shaking hands, his first words were, '*What made you start so soon? did Sis come to Uvalde? I wanted to see them so much.* I brought some presents for *her* & the *children!*' I soon told him all about it for nearly all the passengers had gone to dinner & we had a good time to talk. His presents consisted of a Jar of Ginger preserves for yourself & apples, oranges, almonds, raisons, & candies for the children. I know it would have given him so much pleasure to have given them to you & the babies & that the ginger preserves were the very things you wanted & wished *so much* you could have got them but they will keep & you must come when you can & get them.

Rather than returning to Victoria County, Martha and Thomas remained in San Antonio. Earlier, Thomas had driven a herd of cattle there from the Gulf Coast and sold most of them for $19.50 a head. With the proceeds, he repaid with interest a note held by his mother, and then suggested that she use the money to purchase a certain attractive piece of property he knew was for sale. Martha agreed quickly, as she explained to Anna, "for I thought it best to invest a part of the money in *real estate* and make me a *home* for *life*." For one thousand dollars, Martha bought one hundred acres on the Bandera road, about four and a half miles from the San Antonio city limits.[7] As she wrote Anna in late September, Martha stayed with the Sanford family, who ran a dairy in San Antonio, while Thomas and hired help built Martha a new house. While at the Sanfords, Martha visited with the Truman Phelps family, who, like her, had abandoned the Anaqua area to look for opportunity in San Antonio. For some reason, Martha and Anna shared a private opinion that the women of the Phelps family thought too highly of themselves. In a conspiratorial tone, Martha remarked to Anna concerning the Phelpses, "He brought his family out to dine with me last Sunday (for which I did not thank him) but I think she came to solicit pattronage of the *Laundry*, as she has started one. *Only think of it!* don't let it take away your breath! *Honest labor*, you know." Martha also told Anna that Edwin Phelps had received nomination for the legislature from the Anaqua area, and that "Tho's. thinks the 'old lady' will step high now. He means Mollie P. of course. But *Truman* seems to think it is no honor." Martha's letter contained news about other former Victoria area residents who had recently left the lowlands in search of a healthier place to live. The Wellingtons' hired hand, John Brady, had accompanied them to San Antonio and helped them establish their new farm there. When Thomas Wellington had boarded the train in San Antonio on his way to Uvalde to meet Martha, he had discovered among the passengers the Stoners' former neighbor and relative, James L. Gartrell, who was then traveling through western South Texas looking for land. Also, Martha wrote, Joe and Nannie Jordan left the Stoners' old neighborhood in Victoria County for a new home in West Texas. At the Presbyterian church in San Antonio, Martha ran into her former acquaintance, Reverend Johnson, of Victoria, who rode a circuit from Victoria to Montell, preaching each Sunday in a different location. Also, the Wellingtons anticipated a visit from Amanda Williams, who was a patient of San Antonio physician Ferdinand Herff.[8] When Amanda arrived, Martha hoped to learn more about an incident in the Anaqua area which caused the disbanding of the local school. She told Anna the school "is broken up" because the teacher "went to a 'nigger' ball & danced with the coloured ladies & the people would not send to him again."

In closing her long, informative letter to Anna, Martha asked, "Have you seen the Comet? Look out to the East before Sun rise & if the Mountain is not in the way you will see its tail sticking straight up in the sky." Having just left her daughter's family after five months in the upper Nueces River canyon and having left forever her longtime home on the coastal plain, Martha felt somewhat homesick in her new surroundings in San Antonio. However, the change wrought remarkable, if temporary, benefits for Thomas. "Your Bro's health is better," Martha wrote Anna, "and he seems to be 'wide awake' to the times. He is more altered in business matters than I ever expected him to be—rises a little before day every morning & has every one (except me) stirring." With so many changes occurring so quickly, Martha promised Anna to "keep a Journal to talk to you on & when I fill a sheet, enclose it & mail it," and urged her daughter, in return, "Write to me when ever you can & tell me all the smart things the babies have done & said since I left for it seems a year instead of two weeks" [25 September 1882].

The week after she wrote Anna, Martha moved into her new home just outside San Antonio. In addition to the house, Thomas and his hands built a henhouse and grain house. Their cistern filled quickly and Thomas built a watering tank for the livestock. The property was covered with mesquite, scrub oak, and grass, and crossed by a creek. Besides planning to fence

153

pasture for their own livestock, Martha and Thomas planned to advertise part of the land nearest the creek as a wagon yard, where travelers on the busy San Antonio–Bandera road could pasture their horses overnight for a nominal fee. Desiring to take further advantage of passing traffic, Thomas built a small structure near the road, where he intended to sell groceries and beer. Writing Anna of his plans in early October, Thomas complained that poor health prevented his doing all that he wanted to do. "I am now trying to make a comfortable as well as a profitable home for Ma & I," wrote Thomas, "& I truly hope that I may be able to suceed in my attempt. . . . As to myself I fear that it will be many months or perhaps years before I will see a well day" [7 October 1882].

To increase his mother's comfort, Thomas returned to Victoria County in October 1882 to bring her furniture to their new home. Illness prevented his taking the time to hire extra wagons, so he only took what he could carry in a hack and one wagon. He sold some heavier furnishings, such as his mother's stove, and left the beds, sewing machine, silver, and other family belongings in Amanda Williams's care.[9] Thomas's illness puzzled Martha, who expressed her concern to Anna upon his return from Victoria County:

> I do not know what to think of the disease, nor how to treat it but have been trying the Camphor & kerosine Linament rubed on the lower part of the back where the most of the pain sees to be seated. He says it releives him for the time & I hope it will cure him. He reminds me more and more of your Papa every day in the complication of his complaints & his general appearance. [23 October 1882]

Later, Anna offered her mother another liniment recipe to try on Thomas, one taken from the *Stock Journal* that was originally a cure for black leg in cattle: "Mix equal parts of turpentine & good vinegar, to a pint of the mixture add two table-spoonsfull of salt, & then beat in two eggs; rub the parts effected thoroughly" [5 November 1882]. Because of Thomas's continued poor health, Martha Wellington decided that she needed an income independent of her son. She requested from Anna and Clinton a loan of one hundred dollars to buy sheep and goats. She offered to pay ten percent annual interest for two years and to compose a formal note, if the letter itself was insufficient evidence of the terms. She explained that in San Antonio all purchases required cash payment and that the banks charged much higher interest than she could pay. Martha knew that Clinton and Anna had saved money at Burkett's store in Uvalde. She hoped that they would see the value of earning interest on their savings by loaning part of it to her and admonished them: "Please do not disappoint me if you still have the money, for I cannot ask such a favor of strangers." Added to Martha's anxiety over Thomas's health and her own financial security was concern for her grandchildren's safety on the frontier. The Wellingtons had received a letter from Anna no longer extant in which Anna sent news that Clinton had killed a panther, or mountain lion, near their house. Martha responded to the news, "What did the children say about it? Don't let one of those old things catch granma's babies. Tell Hope not to take Royal off from the house, for old ugly panthers will catch the babies" [23 October 1882].

While Martha and Thomas made a new start in Bexar County, Anna and Clinton became well settled in Edwards County. Laying aside the quilting that occupied most of her extra time that fall, Anna wrote her mother on an October evening after the children were in bed. Responding to Martha's comments about the Phelps family, Anna wrote, "I am sorry to hear Mrs. Truman P. has got to the wash tub but I suppose she has hired hands to do the work for her. I am glad to hear of Edwin's lift, but I am very much afraid he will not be elected."[10]

During October, the Stoners had visitors, and Anna's narrative about them occupied most of her letter. Her story began earlier that month when Reverend Richard Galbraith of the Church of England entered the upper Nueces River canyon looking for land. Word reached Galbraith in his native Ireland that the high, arid plains of the Edwards Plateau were a healthy, prosperous place to emigrate, and he and his son Richard Cecil entered Texas in September 1882, after first visiting Iowa and Missouri. From San Antonio, the two men traveled to Uvalde, and from there to the Nueces River canyon, where they visited the home of an Irish immigrant named Boid, whom Anna wrote was "a nephew of the Episcopal Bishop of Derric in Ireland." Anna emphasized to her mother her impression that Galbraith and Boid were both *"jentry* in the old country." About the Galbraiths, she wrote: "I never saw more pollished gentlemen in all my life they *show* their 'raising' shure and *show* that they are just what the old mans high reccomendations says he is." Boid told Galbraith and his son about the availability of land farther north in the canyon, and the two men procured horses and traveled as far as Dixie, where the minister held religious services the next Sunday. Reaching Bull Head the next day, the men talked with the postmaster, Wells, who gave them a letter of introduction to Clinton. Arriving at the Stoner ranch, the Galbraiths found Clinton hard at work, so they immediately joined him in the fields and helped haul pumpkins to feed hogs. The elder Galbraith left his son with Clinton and Anna during October while he looked for land and again in the winter when he returned to Ireland for the rest of his family. "I dont know what they will do here," Anna told her mother, "unless they bring their servants with them for this boy says they (the ladies) have never done any thing but embroider & such light work as that." Likewise, Richard and Cecil Galbraith were not accustomed to hard, manual labor, but when they visited the upper canyon, according to Anna, they "helped do *any* thing." The younger man's hands were "soft and white" when he arrived, Anna wrote, and after helping Clinton dig and haul twenty-five bushels of potatoes and gather and haul five or six wagonloads of pumpkins, his hands were "covered with blisters" and "hurt most frightfully." Anna described for her mother an incident concerning young Galbraith, and her misspelling of the word *Wales* heightened the humor of her narrative:

> This morning he undertook to get a bucket of water so he went to the rock that you fished over by the spring house diped the bucket into the river & then the poor fellow coul'nt get it out. it sliped out of his hands & then he 'got into the water after it;' as we had a light frost last night & this hapened about sun rise this morning & when we saw that man comeing from the river driping with water you need not think I did'nt laugh for I would have laughed at the Prince of Whales. [20 October 1882]

In a letter to Thomas twelve days later, Anna reported that Richard Galbraith had located property three miles below the Stoners. Along with the land, Galbraith purchased the stock and produce of the former owner, which Clinton and Cecil Galbraith gathered and hauled to the Stoners' place for safekeeping. At the end of October, the elder Galbraith held services at Bull Head and Clinton, Anna, and their children attended [1 November 1882].

In addition to introducing her mother and brother to the Galbraiths, Anna reported in her letters on the health and activities of her family. To Martha, Anna boasted that Hope and Royal were both well and improving in their speech [20 October 1882]. To Thomas, she teased, "the children are as bad as ever and a little wors too" [1 November 1882]. The Stoners now had over one hundred chickens, and Anna discovered the advantages of feeding them Egyptian wheat, or chicken feed, which the previous owners of their land left planted in a small plot behind the smoke house. Clinton bought the twenty-one

Essex hogs included in the purchase of Galbraith's land, which, added to his own Noland hogs, gave him a total of thirty-six hogs to fatten for winter butchering. In the fall of 1882, all but four of Ammon Billings's cows weaned their calves, so the Stoners had less milking to do and less butter to enjoy. The Stoners repaid Billings for his generosity by watching over his farm and family while he spent eighteen days in Gillespie County helping his older brother move to the canyon. During rare moments of leisure, the Stoners read newspapers and magazines received by mail. Among the papers they read during 1882 were the *San Antonio Express* and *Texas Siftings*, the latter a digest of literature, humor, and fashion news from other publications. Thomas Wellington forwarded these publications to the Stoners after he himself read them. Among the magazines Anna and Clinton read was the *Stock Journal*, which informed them of progressive methods of stock tending.

In their earlier letters, both Martha and Thomas had encouraged the Stoners to consider leaving the canyon and moving near them in Bexar County, to which Anna responded in November to Thomas:

> Some how it does not seem to me that I'de like to live there & I am becomeing more & more pleased with this place all the time. Of course I am like you I'de be so glad to be near you and if I thought it would benefit us and our children I would be in for it, but we are fixed now & have plenty to live on & more too and it would be a great sacrifice for us to sell out & move.

Before she received her mother's request for a loan to buy goats, Anna herself suggested to Thomas that he begin raising goats. Through their short experiment with goat raising, the Stoners had learned much about the business, and Anna advised her brother:

> I think if you had some fine goats & some common, so you could have meat from the common ones & shear the fine

ones then you would be fixed the finer your goats are the less apt you are to have twin kids so you see your common goats would be apt to increase faster but that would be all the better for then you could sell off your old nannies & your wethers to the butchers, unless you wanted to butcher them yourself then you would get the hide and tallow.

However, Anna cautioned Thomas against raising goats and hogs together. Thomas would have to keep them separated, especially during spring kidding season, because hogs ate newborn kids if given the chance [1 November 1882].

When Clinton carried Anna's letter of 1 November to the Bull Head post office, he picked up her mother's letter of 23 October containing her request for a loan to buy goats. Anna prefaced her reply to Martha's financial request with the expression, "It is with a heavy heart that I write to you." Clinton and Anna no longer had sufficient cash at Burkett's to supply Martha Wellington's loan. When Richard Galbraith left the upper canyon in late October to locate land and stock for his own family, Clinton gave him two hundred dollars to purchase goats to increase the Stoners' herd. Galbraith did not go far before he located land to buy only three miles down the canyon from Clinton and Anna. Because the land would go to someone else if Galbraith did not buy it immediately, he asked Clinton to purchase the land for him and to hold it as security while he continued his trip to buy Clinton's goats. Clinton wrote a check on his account at Burkett's to the seller, named Colwell, for $260 for the land and twenty-one hogs, twenty bushels of corn, one crib of rye, one stack of hay, one rick of sorghum cane, several plows, and one bee hive. He planned to keep the hogs and half the farm produce to make up most of the sixty dollars difference between the cost of the goats and the cost of the land. After explaining the circumstances to her mother, Anna professed, "Every time I think of it I wish your letter had come the week before it did for Oh you dont know how it hurts me not to be able to send you the money but I do hope brother can get it some where else." The Stoners had allocated what little cash remained in their account in Uvalde for needed improvements to their house. On Clinton's upcoming trip into town, Anna reported, he planned to purchase planks for flooring, a stove for Anna's kitchen, and "what dry goods & groceries we will need through the winter & in fact for all next year maybe" [5 November 1882].

Upon receiving Anna's reply to her loan request, Martha Wellington wrote a letter to her daughter that has since been lost, but to which Anna soon responded, "I can assure you it was a great relief to know you were not so much disappointed as I was afraid you would be." Also in her letter, Anna shared with Martha news from their mutual acquaintances in Victoria County: the Jordans, Crawfords, and Venables. Anna had received a letter from Nannie and Joe Jordan, who migrated to Brady, Texas, in McCulloch County, with the Harvey and Miller families. From Brady, Nannie Jordan wrote Anna, telling her that in her frontier location she was "liveing in a tent and fiteing with the dirt." Her son Walter, she wrote, "plays in the dirt until he is just the coller of the ground dogs." Anna had heard also from Clinton's cousin, Nannie H. Stoner Crawford, who sent fifteen dollars in payment for the stove Clinton and Anna left behind in Victoria County. Nannie informed Anna that most of the Stoner family members in the lowlands, who continued to suffer one illness after the other, had gradually moved from the Stoner Pasture Company compound near Kemper's Bluff, leaving the daily operation of the family business in the hands of George Overton Stoner and his sons. Nannie and James moved into Goliad, where their sons, Michael and Wilkerson, attended school. Anna also told Martha that she and Clinton had received a letter from their former neighbor, Sydney Venable, inquiring about the prospects of his brother Paul's settling in the Nueces River canyon. Responding to the "glowing account" of Uvalde County given them by Maria Stoner Lynn, the Venables sought an escape from the lowlands and the illnesses that continued to plague them there. In his letter, Sydney confirmed the fact that families in the Stoners' former neighborhood were moving away one by one.[11] With the funds from the sale of the old stove, Anna wrote Martha, Clinton had purchased a new Farmer Girl brand wood stove in Uvalde. After Clinton completed his semiannual business at Burkett's store, the kind storekeeper gave him a china doll for Hope. Unfortunately, though, Anna wrote, "before she had it a week she droped it on the hearth & broke it" [22 November 1882].

Before Thanksgiving 1882, Anna received a letter from Thomas stating that, like his health, his financial condition continued to weaken. He had not yet raised the money to stock his store. While he accepted the fact that Clinton and Anna could not help him financially, Thomas inquired about the possibility of obtaining a loan from Clinton's father in Illinois. Thomas requested three hundred dollars to buy grocery stock for the unopened store, to purchase the livestock Martha requested, and to repay the debt he and his mother had previously incurred in Victoria County. He said that he would travel to the canyon to sign for the loan in Clinton's own house, if required, and, as collateral, Thomas offered Thomas Chilton Stoner half of his mother's newly purchased land [22 November 1882].

Upon receipt of Thomas's request, Anna again began her reply, "It is with a very heavy heart that I write to you today." The elder Stoners had decided to use all their spare money to cover expenses for a trip to Texas. When she realized that Clinton's relatives could not make the loan, Anna asked Richard Galbraith to loan Thomas the money. Galbraith would, he said, but wanted twelve percent interest on a one-year loan of three hundred dollars. Also, he required that Thomas pay expenses for a lawyer to write papers on the loan and determine the value of the fifty acres Thomas offered as security. Anna advised Thomas to think carefully before incurring such a debt and suggested that he sell his place in San Antonio, where costs were so high, and move to the canyon, where the possibility still existed to live debt-free:

> Of course you will not have as good society as you find there, but what difference does society do you when your mind is harrassed to death! besides you then have a chance to make something so that some time when you *do go in society* you can look it in the face.

Anna encouraged her brother to move to the canyon quickly, because it was becoming "so thickly settled below here that from Bullhead down to round mountain you never get out of sight of houses besides the houses that you cant see." Furthermore, she added, "they are good people that are moveing in now." The increase in population created disagreements about land boundaries, Anna wrote. Certain newcomers attempted to prove illegal the surveys along the Nueces River, which frequently changed course, thereby widening some settlers' claims while narrowing others. Settlers called for a resurvey of the river lands. Because the Nueces was over thirty feet wide and therefore legally designated a river, the survey determined that property lines of settlers along the river ran to the river's edge, wherever that edge occurred at a given time. After the completion of the survey, settlers already living on the disputed lands received the right of preemption. Anna advised Thomas to bring goats to the canyon, not cattle or sheep:

> I do wish you were here now to get one or two or three places that I know of & if this is a hard winter there will be lots of cattle men leaving here, then I expect one could get disireable places for little or nothing, as every one thinks that the grass will be short for cattle or sheep but fortunately for us goats live on brush & every thing.

By now, Anna and Clinton had financial problems of their own. In mid-November the Reverend Galbraith returned from the trip on which he was to buy goats for Clinton without the goats but with Clinton's two hundred dollars. Most of the money went immediately to Burkett's to pay for the building materials and dry goods Clinton purchased earlier that month. Anna hoped that the little remaining cash would enable her to have ten decayed teeth filled. Until she could have the dental work done, Anna kept bluestone, or blue vitriol, in her mouth to ease the discomfort. In terms of their prospects for the next year, Anna added as a postscript to her letter to Thomas:

> Next Sept. Clinton will have to pay Bob [Stoner] the 300 dollars he ows him & I just dont know how he will do it unless he sells his wether goats at Uvalde for fresh meat if the market there is as good next year as it is now he can raise it easily but I do not know yet how that will be. [29 November 1882][12]

In response to Anna's letter, Thomas Wellington decided against borrowing money from Galbraith; as a result, Thomas never opened his store on the Bandera road.[13]

Since April, when Clinton's father left the canyon, Anna and Clinton had expected a return visit by Thomas Chilton Stoner. He left intent upon selling part of his Illinois farm and renting out the rest in order to return to Texas with his wife, Nancy, son Bob, and daughters Nancy and Mattie. The Stoners hoped to escape the cold Illinois winter by spending several months in western South Texas, a decision influenced by reports of the healthful climate received from their niece, Maria Stoner Lynn, as well as from Anna. After a serious crop failure in the fall of 1882, the train fare to Uvalde liquidated all the family's cash assets. Upon their arrival just before Christmas, Clinton met them with his wagon at the train station and carried them over the rough terrain to his home among the mountains of

163

Edwards County. Although their celebration was not as boisterous as the year before when they had lived with the Joneses, Anna and Clinton spent Christmas 1882 entertaining Clinton's parents and brother and sisters. At thirteen and nine years of age respectively, Nannie and Mattie Stoner were "too big," Anna later wrote her mother, to enjoy the simple Santa Claus candies Anna and Clinton gave Hope and Royal, but the girls presented each of their younger cousins a wax doll with imitation hair [7 January 1883].

Clinton's family stayed in the upper canyon from December 1882 to March 1883 and then spent another month in Texas visiting relatives in Victoria County. This family visit provided Anna's first personal experiences with her mother-in-law, even though they had corresponded for five years. During the months Nancy Hathaway Stoner spent in the canyon, Anna's mind was preoccupied with Thomas Wellington's declining health, and her letters during that period reveal nothing of her impression of her husband's family. After the elder Stoners left the canyon, however, Anna confided to Thomas, "I do not think as much of his mother and sisters as I did before I saw them" [21 March 1883]. When Nancy H. Stoner later reflected upon her time in the canyon, she wrote Clinton, "This has been a hard winter on me and I feel my life is but a span" [9 April 1883]. She frequently grumbled in her letters of problems related to menopause, of fainting spells, and of heart problems. Anna, who seldom, if ever, complained, had found her mother-in-law's presence an added burden in her own work-filled days.

As 1882 drew to a close, the improved health the Stoners sought in the West became a reality for Anna and the children. Anna's only ailment was her decayed teeth and the neuralgia they caused, and she quickly cured what few colds and chills her children experienced. Clinton, however, contracted a cold during his December 1882 ride to the Uvalde railroad station to meet his arriving parents. Although the weather was warm when he began his trip, a sudden norther, like the one that had surprised him on the bear hunt the year before, again caught him unprepared, without shelter or warm clothing. The cold settled in his lungs and he was unable to work for six weeks. During the early months of 1883, Clinton's illness plus the deterioration of Thomas Wellington's health overshadowed the daily life of the Stoner household and dampened the spirit of well-being they had experienced since their arrival in Edwards County.

Letters from a Heavy Heart
January–March 1883

In January 1883, Thomas Wellington sent Anna a postcard informing her to address her next letters to him at his new place of employment, the store of Sauer and Smith, on the corner of Houston and Soledad streets in San Antonio [6 January 1883]. Before receiving the card, Anna wrote her mother with news that she had heard that Major Wells might give up his store and post office at Bull Head. She suggested that Thomas consider taking over Wells's stock and opening his own store in Bull Head. Also, she wrote, the settlers at Hackberry hoped that someone would open a store and post office in their area [7 January 1883]. A few weeks later, Anna wrote Thomas again, reiterating the favorable prospects for Thomas's taking over the Bull Head store. According to Anna, about a dozen families lived in the eight miles between her home and Bull Head, all of whom depended on the post office and store at Bull Head [20 January 1883]. Thomas did not respond to Anna's suggestion, and when she wrote him again in mid-February, a man named Sweeten had moved into the Bull Head area with the intention of putting in a store. Anna complained, "This country is continually settling up untill I think they will be too thick too thrive." Among the newcomers were Button Sánchez, whose mother Anna had met at the Fourth of July celebration in Bull

Head. Sánchez and his brother-in-law named Burns claimed land directly across the Nueces River from Clinton and Anna. The Stoners suspected that the men were on their tract and summoned the surveyor, Mr. Nolan, to mark the corners of their property [10 February 1883].

When Anna next heard from her mother, Martha and Thomas had reached a decision: they would move to the canyon. Thomas wanted to travel through the canyon peddling, perhaps as a sales representative of Sauer and Smith. They received an offer from a German neighbor, Mr. Baker, for their place on the Bandera road, and Martha began doing her own washing "to practice for being in the canyon." One motivation for the Wellingtons' move was to get safely out of the environs of San Antonio, which was in the midst of a smallpox epidemic. Martha herself vaccinated Thomas, and "it *took* slightly, but sufficient," she told Anna. Thirteen deaths had occurred in the city on one Sunday in February, "some from Neumonia," Martha reported, and the city placed "all the S. Pox patients in the Hospital or Pest House." The distraught mother added,"I suppose that is the way they get rid of the S.P. put them in an Hospital or Pest House to prevent its spreding & they soon end their days in there & are buried." Martha confessed that she had begun to dislike living near a growing city, becoming "so full of strangers and so many are invalids with pulminory complaints come from the North to spend the Winter in the South." Thomas, she reported, went into town only as far as Sauer and Smith's store and did as much business by telephone as he could to avoid catching the smallpox [12 February 1883].

Planning their move to the Nueces River canyon helped Thomas and Martha Wellington pass the month of February 1883, while Clinton and Anna prepared for their first kidding season in the canyon. For most of the year, goats required little or no attention. They were hardy enough to withstand the coldest days of winter and found sufficient forage year-round, so that they never required feeding. But in the early weeks of March, kidding season began, when, in Anna's words, "*all* hands will have to attend them." Anna explained to Martha that as soon as a kid could walk, it must be staked to the ground with a soft rope or leather thong tied around one hind foot. Every day, the stake was shifted from one hind foot to another. While they waited for kidding to begin, the Stoners started their spring planting. In spite of two heavy snows, the only losses they suffered were their potatoes; their goats, hogs, and chickens survived. Also, Anna reported, Bull Head no longer had a post master, because Major Wells died on 12 February [17 February 1883].

In March, just after Clinton's family left the canyon and in the midst of kidding season, Anna wrote Thomas that she and Clinton had 220 staked kids and 150 nannies yet to kid. Of the staked kids, they had to feed twenty-one. To Anna's distress, at least thirty-five kids had died, including two billies she believed were worth twenty-five dollars each. "It seems that all of the finest kids die," she wrote sorrowfully. Besides dealing with the goats, Clinton was busy with his planting. Anna reported that he had about ten acres of corn and one acre of oats planted, but the weeds grew faster than the plants. The Nueces River overflowed that month, reaching ten feet up the bank into Anna's garden and carrying away the springhouse. Anna estimated the height of the rise by the drift left in the brush on the side of the cliff under her house. Clinton accomplished much during March 1883 with the newly born kids and freshly planted crops, but he lost days of work at a time because of the lingering effects of the chest cold contracted in December. A worried Anna wrote Thomas, "it may yet end up in consumption as he is still spitting up" [21 March 1883].

While Anna and Clinton tended their goats and their crops in the canyon, Martha and Thomas Wellington suffered further financial distress in San Antonio. Throughout February, the weather remained dry, and the water in their cistern was insufficient for washing clothes, forcing the Wellingtons to pay a laundry in San Antonio one dollar per dozen pieces. Continued drought created a scarcity of forage, and they had to purchase feed for their eight head of cattle and five horses. Then, a horse stepped on Thomas Wellington's foot. A healthy individual would have recovered eventually, but such injuries cause severe infection in persons with diabetes. When Thomas wrote his sister in early March 1883, he reported suffering a severe attack of dropsy, in which, he said, "both my legs and feet were a good deal swolen and the swelling went up one of my legs to my body and in to my bowels." In what became his last letter to Anna, Thomas pleaded with her to come see him, writing:

> I do wish you would come! Come! Come! If possible. I want to see you all so much. . . . I don't believe that I shall ever get well. I may linger along for many years and perhaps not many months or days there is no telling. [6 March 1883]

During March 1883, Martha Wellington continued to seek cures for Thomas and to encourage him to think positively. She studied her husband's medical books and from them learned to make a tonic of iron and camphor, a solution Royal Wellington had administered often in place of quinine. In the evenings when Thomas returned home from Sauer and Smith's, his mother rubbed his swollen feet with camphor liniment and the swelling temporarily subsided. Her encouragements, however, often failed to raise Thomas's spirits. To Anna, she remonstrated, "I have had *so* much trouble trying to convince him that he was improving for if he could once be made to believe it he would be more cheerful which would aid in his recovery." Martha Wellington wrote those words on Friday, 23 March, but during the next few days, Thomas became very ill. The frantic mother penned what was to become her last extant correspondence with her daughter. To her letter begun the previous week, she added the following:

> Since the above was written your poor bro. has grown worse and I am afraid he is in the last stage of his dreadful malidy. Oh my dear Nannie what am I to do? I have tried so hard to believe he was getting better but signs for the worse are too plain. . . . My child *can* you *will* you come to us? . . . In *your* trouble my dear child you never appealed to me in vain and now I am in the deepest *trouble* and I know no one here to call on for help. [23 March 1883]

On Saturday, 31 March 1883, thirty-year-old Thomas Ruffin Albert Wellington died. Anna probably did not receive Martha's letter in time to respond before her brother's death. After settling matters in San Antonio, Martha Wellington sought refuge among the mountains with Anna and Clinton and their children, bringing to an end Anna's extant correspondence with her closest family members.

* * * * *

Under increased stress from the added responsibility of comforting Anna and supporting his grieving mother-in-law, Clinton Stoner ignored his own health care. Upon joining her daughter's household in the spring of 1883, Martha Wellington undoubtedly began experimenting with remedies to relieve Clinton's lung ailment contracted the previous fall. One corrective she had sent Anna earlier was a drink made of raw egg and honey, to be taken every morning. Martha probably admonished her son-in-law often about his overworking, as she had told Anna to do in her last letter to the Stoners:

> Take care of him Nannie for he is trying to take care of you & the babies, bless their little souls. . . . What good would riches do him if he kills himself in trying to gain them? Tell him *for the sake of all he holds most dear, for God's sake, dont kill himself at work but take better care* of himself. [23 March 1883]

Throughout the remainder of 1883, while the family mourned the death of Thomas Wellington, Clinton's condition failed to improve, and Anna, once again pregnant, assumed increased responsibilities to keep the ranch going. Little time was left for correspondence. Clinton's mother wrote six letters to the Stoners, each one expressing more concern about the lack of news from them. When the summer of 1883 passed without a letter from Anna, the worried mother addressed a letter to her son alone, excluding Anna from her usual salutation "Dear Children." When no response came, she directed her next letter to her grandchildren, Hope and Royal, who, of course, were too young to reply. By ignoring Clinton and Anna, Nancy Stoner probably hoped to shame her son and daughter-in-law into writing. On 4 February 1884, the Thomas Chilton Stoner family received a telegram from their niece Maria Lynn informing them of the death of their son William Clinton on 30 January. Responding on behalf of the bereaved parents, their friend Moses Walker wrote Maria:

> It greatly dispels the gloom to know Clinton was in his last hours surrounded by friends to sooth his pain and to render him all of the aid possible on this earth. That you were there to console Nannie and the little ones is the greatest comfort to the friends here. Nannie and the children will not be forgotten. [6 February 1884]

Five weeks after Clinton's death, kidding season began among the Stoners' goat herd, and in the midst of that busiest time of year, Anna gave birth to her third child, a son, whom she named after his father. As spring 1884 brought new life to the upper Nueces River canyon, Anna Wellington Stoner and her children faced a new beginning that called forth much courage and strength.

Afterword

On 30 January 1944, eighty-seven-year-old Anna Louisa Stoner, sitting at her kitchen table, began a letter addressed to her children and grandchildren. Her eyesight growing dim, Anna held a magnifying glass between her spectacles and her pen, while she wrote:

> It is sixty years ago today since my husband Wm. Clinton Stoner died, in Edwards Co., about eight miles above Vance on the main Nueces River. A sad sad day for me. No home—no support except a flock of non shearing, common goats of many collors. My oldes[t] child, Hope four years & 9 months old. Royal three years one month & two days old. Little Clinton was born the sixth of March following his fathers death on Jan. 30, 1884. [30 January 1944]

Exhausted from the effort of writing and the emotion of the memory, Anna set aside her pen and left the letter unfinished. The sad, sad day of Clinton's death did not mark the finish of Anna's story any more than her final correspondence marked the end of her influence.

Widowed at age twenty-seven, with two young children, an infant, and an aging mother as dependents, Anna chose to remain in the Nueces River canyon rather than return to the coastal plain. The mountains of the upper Nueces River canyon, which she once believed held promise for becoming a beautiful and pleasant home, now symbolized sorrow, hardship, and danger. Outlaws, still haunting the region, took advantage of her vulnerability and stole her finest horses, and hands hired to help with her goat stock proved untrustworthy. In the fall following Clinton's death, Anna retreated to the lower Nueces River canyon, where longtime friends stood ready to bolster her courage. In September 1884, she sold her home in Edwards County and returned to northwestern Uvalde County, where she bought 320 acres near Round Mountain between the settlements of Montell and Good Luck.[1]

For a while the Stoner family once again lived in a tent, while Anna struggled to make a living by collecting small animal hides, raising goats, and growing corn. She traded the skins for groceries and hardware in Uvalde and sold her mohair to brokers in New York, both for slim profits. A few business receipts from her early days as a widowed rancher reveal the difficulty of her task. Nine coon skins delivered in 1886 to Charles Smidt Dry Goods in Uvalde brought only $1.44, which after being applied to the purchase of soda, canned tomatoes, and twine, left Anna with a credit of forty-nine cents. Her 1886 fall clip of 214 pounds of mohair sold at fifteen cents a pound, but after deductions for freight and handling charges, her proceeds were $27.65, an amount that lowered only slightly her standing account of nearly eighty dollars at F. A. Piper & Company in Uvalde. With thirty-two bushels of corn, valued at seventy-five cents a bushel, Anna paid almost half of her $51 doctor's bill in March 1886. The sympathetic physician, C. L. Whitfield, offered to give Anna as long as she needed to raise the remainder of what she owed.[2]

Upon her return to the lower canyon, Anna received help from friendly neighbors and an occasional hired hand, but for the most part, relied upon her own strength and resourcefulness. Her belief in the power of positive thought, expressed over and over again in her earlier letters to her ailing brother, undoubtedly raised Anna's spirits through hard times. Eventually, Anna reserved enough cash to finance a house, built with prime lumber hauled from San Antonio to a plot of bottom land between the Nueces River and its tributary, Miller Creek. Sporadic aid came from Clinton's family in Illinois. Thomas Chilton Stoner, Sr., visited Anna several times through the years and became especially fond of his son's namesake. Nancy H. Stoner wrote Anna occasionally, but the elder Stoners abandoned their plans to move to Texas. However, thirty-three years after Clinton's death, his brother, Thomas Chilton Stoner, Jr., moved to the lower Nueces River canyon near Anna and raised a family, whose descendants still live there.[3]

Ironically, medical bills became Anna's primary expenses in the same canyon where she once believed no one became ill. Her mother, Martha Elizabeth Wellington, died in Anna's home two days after Christmas 1886 and was buried in the Montell Cemetery. Born a few weeks after her husband's death, Anna's youngest child, William Clinton Stoner, Jr., suffered infantile paralysis and required a physician's frequent care to relieve his pain. Often during the next eighteen years Anna rode horseback alone through the night the fifteen or so miles to fetch the doctor to Clinton, Jr.'s bedside. He was a pale child with a crippled foot and a lovely singing voice, who brought his mother joy until his death on 9 August 1902. Anna buried her youngest child in the Montell Cemetery at the foot of her mother's grave.

The older Stoner children, Hope and Thomas Royal, helped their mother on the ranch as much as their youth allowed. Distance and the pressing needs of the ranch prevented the children from attending school very often or very long. The hardships of her years in the canyon were bitter memories for Hope, and upon her marriage on 17 February 1909, to Edward G. Beaumont, she gladly left Texas for California.[4] Royal decided to make the canyon his permanent home. As he grew into adulthood, he displayed his self-taught cowboy skills at local rodeos and horse races, all the while increasing his mother's goat herd and adding sheep, cattle, and horses to the ranch stock. Over the years, the Stoners added over twenty-six hundred acres to the original ranch land. In 1902 both Anna and Royal became members of the American Angora Goat Breeders Association. Of over three hundred qualified members of the AAGBA, Anna Stoner was the sixth female accepted.[5]

Royal Stoner chose his bride from among his father's Victoria County relatives. On 26 July 1911, he married Mamie Victoria Stoner, daughter of George Overton and Zilpa Rose Stoner. Royal and his bride, like canyon couples before them, erected a tent for their first home. Acquiring land adjacent to his mother's ranch, Royal devoted the rest of his life to running the two ranches. Here the Stoners raised three children, Mary Margaret, Michael Lowery, and Royal Clinton.[6] Anna's grandchildren visited her daily during their childhood and heard tales of their grandfather Clinton and his pioneering efforts in the canyon that was their home. From Anna, they developed a love of reading, and she drew their attention to tales of western adventure in the novels of Zane Grey and the stories of *Frontier Times*. From their mother's parents they learned about their other Stoner relatives, who had made young Clinton welcome when he first arrived in Victoria County. When they left home for college, marriage, and military service, all three grandchildren received letters from Anna, which

Children of William Clinton and Anna Louisa Wellington
Stoner, circa 1889, Austin, Texas. From left, William Clinton
Stoner, Jr.; Thomas Royal Stoner; and Hope Augusta Stoner.
Reproduced by permission of The Texas Collection, Baylor
University, Waco, Texas.

kept them linked with family and home in spite of physical separation.

When Martha E. Wellington had moved to Anna's mountain home in Edwards County following her son's death in 1883, she had carried with her the letters received by her parents in frontier Arkansas beginning in 1831, the letters, journal, and papers of her doctor-husband dating from 1840, correspondence she received from Arkansas after her migration to Texas in 1852, and most of the letters received from her children since 1873. After her mother's death, Anna added to the collection hundreds of postcards, letters, and photographs received from her correspondents throughout the United States. She maintained contact with several generations of Foster, Betts, Nash, and Stoner descendants as well as the children and grandchildren of her childhood friend, Nannie Cromwell Holliday. Anna placed the treasured letters in an old trunk, which she kept beside an oak dining table in the front room of her home near the Nueces River. One night in 1913, a sudden rush of flood waters created by a rain upstream threatened to overrun the site where Anna's house stood. Royal and Mamie abandoned their nearby tent and helped Anna secure her furnishings against the rising waters. Anna placed the trunk filled with family treasures on top of the dining table and took refuge with Royal and Mamie in a tall pecan tree behind the house. The next morning, the Stoners discovered Anna's house several hundred yards downstream, wedged between two large trees. The table and trunk inside had floated to the ceiling but had not escaped out the door. Although covered in silt, the family letters remained intact to be passed on to future generations, to whom they serve as reminders of the struggles endured and sacrifices made in order to maintain family ties.

As Anna grew older and the extent of the historical transitions experienced during her lifetime grew in significance, her collection of family letters provided a tangible link with the past. The written expressions of real persons being themselves in ordinary circumstances, the letters capture the historical moment in a way that allows the eyes of the present to view commonplace events through the eyes of the past. Modernization and technology gradually reached the Nueces River canyon in the twentieth century, altering the landscape and changing forever the everyday experiences of ranching families, and the story of Anna Stoner's struggle for survival blended with other pioneer tales to become part of the region's cultural identity.[7] On her eightieth birthday, in an especially fitting gesture of friendship, Anna's longtime neighbors wrote her letters filled with remembrances of her life. Obediah D. "Doc" Coleman, whose family's ranch was just north of Round Mountain, was a teenager when Anna and her children settled on their Uvalde County land. Dictating Anna's birthday message to his daughter, Coleman recalled his earliest and latest memories of his neighbor and friend in the following manner:

> Looking back, I remember you when I first knew you, a young mother with three little babies, who had just recently lost a loving father and you a devoted husband. Well do I remember the hardships that you underwent and the daily struggle to raise your little ones. But always, no matter what the day brought forth, you met every trial with a smile.
>
> There have been many days go by since that time and much water has run under the bridge. But it has failed to wash away the smile and cheerful words of comfort to everyone. I can truthfully say you are the same loving mother and friend I knew long, long ago.
>
> Would we go back and live again the same life? Yes, for there are sweet memories as well as the sad ones always to repay one for every trial.[8]

Always pragmatic, Anna maintained an avid interest in the day-to-day operation of her ranch until her death on 10 July

1953 at the age of ninety-six and a half years. She died on the ranch she founded and was buried beside her mother and son in Montell Cemetery. Thomas Royal Stoner was seventy-three years old when he inherited his mother's ranch.[9] Within a few years, he gave control of the Stoner Ranch to his children. His sons purchased their sister's third of the land and operated the ranch as partners from 1957 to 1960, when Michael, having purchased a ranch of his own on the Frio River, sold his half of the land to his brother Royal. In 1984 the Texas Department of Agriculture recognized the Stoner Ranch as a Family Land Heritage Ranch, a distinction reserved for ranches operated continuously by the founder's descendants for at least a century. The following year, Anna's grandchildren presented her family letters and ranching papers to The Texas Collection, Baylor University, Waco, Texas.

Just as they bonded Anna with her mother and brother from 1873 to 1883, the letters of Anna Wellington Stoner connect readers in the late twentieth century with the indefatigable spirit of one nineteenth-century South Texas woman and her family. Like Anna, women continue to face life-changing events. Some changes require only the application of traditional knowledge and skills, but others force adaptation and the creation of new ways of coping. Like the Stoners, families are caught up in the historical and cultural transitions of their own era, changes sometimes of their own making but often beyond their control. The Wellington-Stoner letters serve as a reminder that broad historical events, including the settlement of the American West, are made up of myriad ordinary lives, male and female, for whom the basic concerns of everyday life are of primary importance. The more historians discover about their struggles for daily survival, their means of maintaining family continuity, and their ways of mutual cooperation, the more authentic the story of the past will become.

Appendix

Genealogy of Anna Louisa Wellington and William Clinton Stoner

Ancestry of Anna Louisa Wellington Stoner[1]

Williamson Foster
> b. _____ , Prince Edward Co., VA, son of George and Judith Price Foster
> d. 26 November 1848, Spring Hill, Hempstead Co., AR
> m. **Ann Haskins Ligon,** 20 April 1813, Prince Edward Co., VA
> > b. 8 January 1791, Prince Edward Co., VA, daughter of John Turner Ligon, Sr., and Jane Haskins Ligon
> > d. 3 August 1850, Spring Hill, Hempstead Co., AR

Children of Williamson and Ann Ligon Foster:
> 1. Louisa Jane Foster
> 2. George William Foster
> 3. Mary Jane Foster
> 4. John Turner Foster
> 5. Cornelia Ann Foster m. Samuel Burris Fluett
> 6. **Martha Elizabeth Foster** (see below)
> 7. Albert Gallatin Foster
> 8. Benjamin Haskins Foster
> 9. Patrick Henry Foster
> 10. Louisa Virginia Foster m. James Chauncey Harvey Betts

Martha Elizabeth Foster
> b. 14 August 1823, Prince Edward Co., VA
> d. 27 December 1886, Uvalde Co., TX
> m. **Royal Wetherton Wellington,** 23 January 1851, Spring Hill, Hempstead Co., AR
>> b. 18 July 1815, Philadelphia, PA
>> d. 26 March 1875, Refugio Co., TX

Children of Royal W. and Martha E. Foster Wellington:
> 1. Thomas Ruffin Albert Wellington
>> b. 30 August 1852, Saluria, TX
>> d. 31 March 1883, San Antonio, TX
> 2. **Anna Louisa Wellington**
>> b. 17 January 1857, Refugio Co., TX
>> d. 10 July 1953, Montell, Uvalde Co., TX
>> m. **William Clinton Stoner,** 28 November 1877, Refugio Co., TX

Ancestry of William Clinton Stoner[2]

George Washington Stoner
> b. 25 October 1787, Clarke Co., KY, son of George Michael "Old Mike" Stoner and Frances Tribble
> d. 20 June 1871, Mt. Sterling, Montgomery Co., KY
> m. **Nancy Tribble,** 1812, KY
>> b. 20 August 1794, daughter of Mary Boone and Peter Burris Tribble
>> d. 6 December 1872, Mt. Sterling, Montgomery Co., KY

Children of George Washington and Nancy Tribble Stoner:
> 1. Clinton D. Stoner
> 2. Sarah Ann Stoner
> 3. Michael Lowery Stoner
> 4. Mary Ann Stoner
> 5. Peter Tribble Stoner
> 6. Frances Miriam Stoner

7. Minerva Tribble Stoner
8. George Washington Stoner
9. **Thomas Chilton Stoner** (see below)
10. Nancy Tribble Stoner
11. Maria Fox Stoner
12. Robert Gatewood Stoner

Thomas Chilton Stoner
b. 24 March 1829, Kentucky
d. 6 September 1914, Mt. Zion, Macon Co., IL
m. **Nancy Jane Hathaway,** 3 September 1851, Montgomery Co., KY
  b. 3 December 1830, KY
  d. 28 April 1900, Mt. Zion, Macon Co., IL
Children of Thomas Chilton and Nancy Hathaway Stoner:
1. **William Clinton Stoner**
    b. _____ 1852, KY
    d. 30 January 1884, Edwards Co., Texas
    m. **Anna Louisa Wellington,** 28 November 1877, Refugio Co., Texas
2. Andrew Stoner
3. Millard Filmore Stoner
4. Mary Petetta Stoner
5. Thomas Chilton Stoner, Jr.
6. Robert Lee Stoner
7. Nancy Stoner
8. Mattie Allen Stoner

Descendants of
William Clinton and Anna Wellington Stoner

Children:
1. **Hope Augusta Stoner**
    b. 22 April 1879, Victoria Co., TX

d. 13 June 1942, Fresno, CA

m. **Edward G. Beaumont,** 17 February 1909, Montell, Uvalde Co., TX

Children of Hope Augusta and Edward G. Beaumont:
1. **Maide,** b. 29 August 1911, Fresno, CA
2. **Anna Louise,** b. 22 May 1913, Fresno, CA
3. **Hope,** b. 31 December 1916, Fresno, CA

2. **Thomas Royal Stoner**
   b. 28 December 1880, Victoria Co., TX
   d. 28 March 1960, Uvalde Co., TX
   m. **Mamie Victoria Stoner,** 26 July 1911, Victoria Co., TX, daughter of George Overton and Zilpa Rose Stoner
      b. 4 September 1885, Victoria Co., TX
      d. 22 January 1974, Uvalde Co., TX

Children of Thomas R. and Mamie Stoner: (see below)

3. **William Clinton Stoner, Jr.**
   b. 6 March 1884, Edwards Co., TX
   d. 9 August 1902, Uvalde Co., TX

Children of Thomas Royal and Mamie Victoria Stoner:
1. **Mary Margaret Stoner**
   b. 5 June 1915, Victoria, TX
   m. **Malcolm Dallas McLean,** 11 February 1939, Montell, Uvalde Co., TX
      b. 10 March 1913, Rogers, TX

Children of Margaret and Malcolm McLean:
1. **John Robertson McLean**
   b. 21 October 1943, Uvalde, TX
   m. **Ellen Claire Miles,** 3 September 1966, Corpus Christi, TX
      b. 11 August 1943

Children of John R. and Ellen McLean:
1. **Malcolm Hugh McLean**

     b. 10 July 1968, Houston, TX

  2. **Douglas Duncan McLean**

     b. 7 February 1971, Houston, TX

2. **Michael Lowery Stoner**

  b. 14 October 1916, Victoria, TX

  m. (1) Frederica Bonnie Hallaran, 8 July 1958, Bandera, TX

     b. 16 December 1914

     d. 4 December 1965

    (2) Patricia Roann Daugherty Cartwright, 12 October 1987, Concan, Uvalde Co., TX

     b. 28 January 1942, Harris Co., TX

3. **Royal Clinton Stoner**

  b. 25 April 1918, Victoria, TX

  m. **Robbie Mae Scruggs**, 27 December 1958, San Antonio, TX

     b. 13 October 1927

Children of Royal Clinton and Robbie Stoner:

1. **Thomas Overton Stoner** (twin)

  b. 25 September 1959

  m. Jacqueline Dee Curtis, 1 June 1985

     b. 19 September 1961

2. **Gilbert Joseph Stoner** (twin)

  b. 25 September 1959

3. **Jamie Louise Stoner**

  b. 23 July 1961

  m. Bob Louis McCracken, 22 July 1989, Montell, Uvalde Co., TX

     b. 8 July 1954

Notes

Notes to Introduction

[1]See Nancy F. Cott, *Root of Bitterness: Documents of the Social History of American Women* (New York: E. P. Dutton, 1972); Christiane Fischer, ed., *Let Them Speak for Themselves: Women in the American West, 1849–1900* (Hamden, CT: Archor Books, Shoe String Press, 1977); Joan M. Jensen, *With These Hands: Women Working on the Land* (Old Westbury, NY: Feminist Press, 1981); Mary Kelley, ed., *Woman's Being, Woman's Place: Female Identity and Vocation in American History* (Boston: G. K. Hall, 1979); Cathy Lee Luchetti, *Women of the West* (St. George, UT: Antelope Island Press, 1982); Glenda Riley, *Frontierswomen: The Iowa Experience* (Ames: Iowa State University Press, 1981); Lillian Schlissel, *Women's Diaries of the Westward Movement* (New York: Schocken Books, 1982); and Joanna L. Stratton, *Pioneer Women: Voices from the Kansas Frontier* (New York: Simon & Schuster, 1981).

[2]The pioneering work on frontier women's stereotypes was Beverly J. Stoeltje, " 'A Helpmate for Man Indeed': The Image of the Frontier Woman," *Journal of American Folklore* 88 (January-March 1975): 25–41. Other classic studies on stereotypes include Barbara Welter, "The Cult of True Womanhood: 1820–1860," in *The American Family in Social-Historical Perspective*, 2d edition, ed. Michael Gordon (New York: St. Martin's Press, 1978), 313–33; and Joan M. Jensen and Darlis A. Miller, "The Gentle Tamers Revisited: New Approaches to the History of Women in the American West," *Pacific Historical Review* 49 (May 1980): 173–213.

[3]See Julie Roy Jeffrey, *Frontier Women: The Trans-Mississippi West 1840–1880* (New York: Hill & Wang, 1979); John Mack Faragher, *Women and Men on the Overland Trail* (New Haven, CT: Yale University Press, 1979); and Sandra L. Myres, *Westering Women and the Frontier Experience 1800–1915* (Albuquerque: University of New Mexico Press, 1982).

[4]See Susan Armitage and Elizabeth Jameson, eds., *The Women's West* (Norman: University of Oklahoma Press, 1987). Glenda Riley postulated the existence of a separate female frontier based on the homogeneity of western women's gender roles, claiming that women's common experiences transcended natural region, husband's occupation, and historical period, in *The Female Frontier: A Comparative View of Women on the Prairie and the Plains* (Lawrence: University Press of Kansas, 1988). Sharon Niederman found that while women responded individually to westward migration, they shared the challenge of applying their strongest inner resources to meet their situation; *A Quilt of Words: Women's Diaries, Letters and Original Accounts of Life in the Southwest, 1860–1960* (Boulder, CO: Johnson Books, 1988).

[5]Lillian Schlissel concluded that in spite of women's efforts to maintain family continuity, frontier conditions ultimately won out, breaking families apart, in "Families and Frontiers: A Reading for Our Time," in Lillian Schlissel, Byrd Gibbens, and Elizabeth Hampsten, *Far From Home: Families of the Westward Journey* (New York: Schocken Books, 1989), 231–45.

[6]See Mattie Austin Hatcher, *Letters of an Early American Traveler: Mary Austin Holley, Her Life and Her Works, 1784–1846* (Dallas: Southwest Press, 1933); Elise Waerenskjold, *The Lady with the Pen: Elise Waerenskjold in Texas* (Northfield, MN: Norwegian-American Historical Association, 1961; reprint, ed. C. A. Clausen, Clifton, TX: Bosque Memorial Museum, 1976); Crystal Sasse Ragsdale, *The Golden Free Land: The Reminiscences and Letters of Women on an American Frontier* (Austin, TX: Landmark Press, 1976); and Sister Mary Patrick Joseph, *Letters from the Ursuline*

1852–1853: From Our Beloved Sisters Who Quitted St. Mary's, April 17th, 1852, to Commence the Mission at San Antonio, ed. Catherine McDowell (San Antonio, TX: Trinity University Press, 1977). Transcribed letters of other nineteenth-century Texas women are included in Gary Doyle Woods, comp., *The Hicks-Adams-Bass-Floyd-Patillo and Collateral Lines, Together with Family Letters 1840–1868* (Salado, TX: Privately printed, Anson Jones Press, 1963); Marion T. Brown, *Letters from Fort Sill 1886–1887*, ed. C. Richard King (Austin, TX: The Encino Press, 1970); Katherine Hart and Elizabeth Kemp, eds., *Lucadia Pease and the Governor: Letters, 1850–1857* (Austin, TX: The Encino Press, 1974); and David Holman, comp., *Letters of Hard Times in Texas 1840–1890* (Austin, TX: Roger Beacham, 1974).

Notes to Chapter 1

All quoted and paraphrased letters in this book are located in the Wellington-Stoner-McLean Papers, The Texas Collection, Baylor University, Waco, Texas. Within the collection, the papers are filed by date. To facilitate identification of letters, author and recipient both are identified in the text preceding the quoted passage and the quote is then identified by date. In cases where several portions of a single letter are quoted in succession, the date follows the final quoted passage.

[1]The record of Foster family ancestors in Piedmont Virginia appears in Herbert Clarence Bradshaw, *History of Prince Edward County, Virginia* (Richmond, VA: Dietz Press, 1955), 1–21. Foster and Ligon genealogies appear in William D. Ligon, Jr., *The Ligon Family and Connections* (Hartford, CT: Bond Press, 1947).

[2]In the 1830s, an English traveler noted the contrast between the refinements of the Spring Hill settlers and their frontier living environment. See G[eorge] W[illiam] Featherstonhaugh, *Excursion Through the Slave States, from Washington on the Potomac to the Frontier of Mexico; with Sketches of Popular Manners and Geological Notices* (New York: Harper & Brothers, 1844; reprint, New York: Ne

gro Universities Press, 1968), 122–23 (page references are to reprint edition). Another traveler wrote in 1844 that people in Little Rock called the Spring Hill area "the Aristocratic Region." See Francis J. Scully, "Across Arkansas in 1844," *Arkansas Historical Quarterly* 13 (Spring 1954): 40. The founding of the Spring Hill Academy is discussed in Walter Moffatt, "Arkansas Schools, 1819–1840," *Arkansas Historical Quarterly* 12 (Summer 1953): 100–101. Willard's role in advancing the education of young women is presented in Ann Firor Scott, "What, Then, is the American: This New Woman?," *Journal of American History* 65 (December 1978): 679–703. Foster's role in founding Spring Hill Academy was recalled by his granddaughter, Anna Louisa Stoner, in "Explanation," AMsS, 29 April 1940, Wellington-Stoner-McLean Papers, The Texas Collection, Baylor University, Waco, Texas [hereafter referred to as WSM Papers], and is verified in Allen Stokes, "Education in Young Arkansas: Spring Hill Female Academy," *Arkansas Historical Quarterly* 27 (Summer 1968): 113.

[3]Nothing is known about the early death of Mary Jane Foster. Cornelia Foster married planter Samuel Burris Fluett on 31 May 1842. She died two years later and was buried in the Foster family cemetery, three miles west of Spring Hill, Arkansas. See A. R. Banks, "Records of the Springhill Church Session," transcribed by John A. Manry, TMs, Southwest Arkansas Regional Archives, Washington, Arkansas. Louisa V. Foster's marriage was announced in the *Washington (Arkansas) Telegraph*, 31 March 1847.

[4]Information on Wellington's birth and early life is taken from Margaret Stoner McLean, "Biography of Dr. Royal Wetherton Wellington (1815–1874)," TMsS, 17 April 1950, WSM Papers. His various involvements before settling in Arkansas are recorded in his correspondence, WSM Papers.

[5]Ruffin and Wellington maintained correspondence after Ruffin returned to his native North Carolina to practice law and served as representative, United States Congress, 1853–61. He reached the rank of colonel in the First North Carolina Cavalry during the Civil War, was wounded at Bristol Station, and died in prison at Alexandria, Virginia,

on 13 October 1863. Jon L. Wakelyn, *Biographical Dictionary of the Confederacy* (Westport, CT: Greenwood Press, 1977), 375–76.

[6]Wellington kept a ledger of his medical practice in Arkansas from 14 August 1847 to 1 January 1852. See Royal Wetherton Wellington, Journal, AMs, WSM Papers.

[7]"Will of Williamson Foster," transcribed from Hempstead County, Arkansas, Probate Records [photocopy], 10 January 1848, WSM Papers.

[8]Bobbie Jones McLane and Capitola Hensley Glazner, comps., *Hempstead County, Arkansas, Marriage Records, 1817–1875* (Hot Springs, AR: Privately printed, 1969), 156; and Ligon, *Ligon Family*, 719.

[9]Hobart Huson, *Refugio: A Comprehensive History of Refugio County from Aboriginal Times to 1953* (Woodsboro, TX: Rooke Foundation, 1953), 1: 6, 467–68, 529, 548, 553, places physician Royal W. Wellington at Mesquite Landing on the San Antonio River as early as 1842. Evidence from Wellington's journal and personal correspondence, however, indicates that he was in Missouri at that time and did not migrate to Texas until 1852.

[10]The Bible, a valued possession of Wellington's great-granddaughter, Mary Margaret Stoner McLean, Arlington, Texas, remains a repository of family history, most recently extending to the sixth generation.

[11]Bond of Sale, 15 July 1853, WSM Papers; Refugio County, Texas, Transcribed Record of Deeds, D: 300, E: 2, Refugio, Texas. Wellington originally bought the land in partnership with his brother-in-law, C. J. H. Betts, but Betts decided against moving to Texas and sold his half of the deed to Wellington in 1856. Refugio County, Texas, Deeds, E: 244.

[12]Anaqua was situated on the ancient camping ground of the Anaqua Indians, who lived there when Álvar Núñez Cabeza de Vaca named the site. Irish immigrants settling Power and Hewetson's Colony arrived at Anaqua in 1820 and established a trading center, where the first post office was a box nailed to a tree. See Huson, *Refugio*, 1: 7. After the San Antonio River changed course southward in 1936,

the river bed that originally bordered the Wellington land became known as Old River, and its dry channel remains the Victoria-Refugio county line. Editorial Staff of The Handbook of Texas, eds., *The Handbook of Victoria County* (Austin: Texas State Historical Association, 1990), 83.

[13]Wellington maintained his medical accounts in Texas in the same ledger he began in Arkansas. See R. W. Wellington, Journal, AMs, WSM Papers. Brand registration, DS, 17 April 1855, WSM Papers.

[14]A. L. Stoner, "Explanation," AMsS, 20 April 1940, WSM Papers.

[15]Refugio County, Texas, Commissioners Court Minutes, Book 1, 127, Refugio, Texas; Huson, *Refugio*, 2: 7–8.

[16]Tax Receipt, DS, 6 April 1860, WSM Papers; National Archives and Records Services, *Population Schedules of the Eighth Census of the United States, 1860, Texas*, Microcopy 653, Roll 1303 (Washington, DC: National Archives, 1967), 9: 192; and National Archives and Records Services, *Population Schedules of the Eighth Census of the United States, 1860, Texas, Slave Schedules*, Microcopy 653, Roll 1311 (Washington, DC: National Archives, 1967), 2: 305.

[17]J. J. Bowden, *The Exodus of Federal Forces from Texas 1861* (Austin, TX: Eakin Press, 1986), 100–104.

[18]See Huson, *Refugio*, 2: 30–31.

[19]Victor M[arion] Rose, *Some Historical Facts in Regard to the Settlement of Victoria, Texas: Its Progress and Present Status* (Laredo, TX: Daily Times Plant, 1883; republished, J. W. Petty, Jr., ed., Victoria, TX: Book Mart, 1961), 100.

[20]R. W. Wellington, Journal, AMs, WSM Papers.

[21]Huson, *Refugio*, 1: 505; Elizabeth Mainland to M. E. Wellington, 4 November 1864, WSM Papers; and Brownson Malsch, *Indianola: The Mother of Western Texas*, rev. ed. (Austin, TX: State House Press, 1988), 166–67.

[22]Huson, *Refugio*, 2: 11; and Roy Grimes, ed., *300 Years in Victoria County* (Victoria, TX: Victoria Advocate, 1968), 267.

[23]Hobart Huson, "Two Sea Captains Johnson and Some of Their Friends," 1 December 1958, TMsS, Victoria Public Library, Victoria, Texas.

[24]Lease agreement, ADS, January 1866, WSM Papers; R. W. Wellington, Journal, AMs, WSM Papers. While Wellington hired freedmen, some of his neighbors resented emancipation and the fact that a black federal regiment occupied the town of Victoria. See Charles W. Ramsdell, "Presidential Reconstruction in Texas," *The Quarterly of the Texas State Historical Association* 12 (January 1909): 221–22. Racial violence struck close to the Wellingtons in July 1866, when Alexander Cromwell, the son of their neighbor Alexander Hawkins Cromwell, killed a freedman and fled the state to avoid arrest. Following Reconstruction, Cromwell returned to Victoria, confessed to the murder, and received acquittal when no witnesses appeared against him. *The Victoria (Texas) Advocate*, 17 November and 24 November 1877.

[25]Tax Receipts, 27 July 1866; 15 July 1867; 15 February, 17 February, 1 August, and 27 September 1868; 16 September and 20 November 1869; 24 March, 15 November, and 13 December 1871; 4 July 1872; 22 September and 15 November 1873, WSM Papers.

[26]Refugio County, Texas, Deeds H: 45–48.

[27]National Archives and Records Services, *Population Schedules of the Ninth Census of the United States, 1870, Texas*, Microcopy 593, Roll 1602 (Washington, DC: National Archives, 1965), 16: 138.

[28]A. L. Stoner, ANS, 10 January 1938, WSM Papers.

[29]Receipt, DS, September 1868, WSM Papers. Grimes, *Victoria County*, 539, 541. All comprehensive histories of Victoria County refer to Mrs. Case's Victoria Female Academy. The most detailed account is the chapter entitled "History of the Bronte Literary Club, Oldest Existing Woman's Club in Texas," in Leopold Morris, *Pictorial History of Victoria and Victoria County* (San Antonio, TX: Clemens Printing Co., 1953), [47–54].

[30]Receipt, DS, 3 January 1870, WSM Papers.

[31]A copy of the textbook, published in 1866, signed and dated by Thomas and Anna on 14 April 1869 at Victoria, is among the archival materials of the WSM Papers.

[32]Invitation, 19 August 1869, WSM Papers; Margaret Stoner

McLean, "Tournaments: An Account of This Early Sport in Victoria, Texas, and Neighboring Communities," *The Cattleman* 35 (September 1948): 48–49, 188–92. Anna's granddaughter recalled that Anna always wore gloves and carried a handkerchief to public events because the stress of such occasions caused her hands to perspire. See Mary Margaret McLean, Oral Memoirs of Mary Margaret Stoner McLean, typed transcript of a series of tape-recorded interviews conducted by Lois E. Myers, in progress, Baylor University Institute for Oral History, Waco, Texas.

[33]Steven M. Stowe traces similar emotional tensions expressed in letters between two Southern parents and their adolescent daughter in "Growing Up Female in the Planter Class," *Helicon Nine: The Journal of Women's Arts and Letters* (Spring 1987)): 195–205.

[34]The Convent School, opened in 1867 by the Monastery of the Incarnate Word and Blessed Sacrament, later became known as Nazareth Academy and received recognition as a superior school for women. Editorial Staff, *Handbook*, 71.

[35]The Bluffs, frequently referred to in the Wellington correspondence, was Kemper's Bluff, located on the west side of the Guadalupe River eight miles east of Anaqua. Founded by John Frederick Kemper in the 1830s, Kemper's Bluff rivaled Victoria in importance as the terminus of steamship traffic on the river until 1845, when a party of Karankawa Indians raided the trading post and killed Kemper. Local families continued to refer to the site as the Bluffs even after it became a registered post office with the name Kemper City. George Overton Stoner served as the postmaster of Kemper City in 1883 and 1907, and between those years the town relocated five miles west. See National Archives and Records Administration, *Post Office Department Reports of Site Locations, 1837–1950*, Microfilm Publication M1126 [photocopy] (Washington, DC: National Archives and Records Administration, n.d.).

[36]Wellington's death date was recorded by his wife in the same family Bible in which she had recorded her children's births. Beginning 27 March 1875, Thomas Wellington maintained a ledger of the expenses

of his father's estate. See T. R. A. Wellington, "General Account of Expenditures of the Family of R. W. Wellington, Dec'd," AMsS, WSM Papers. See also Refugio County, Texas, Probate Records, R. W. Wellington, Refugio, Texas. The Wellington estate brand is recorded in Victoria County, Texas, Mark and Brand Book 1, Victoria, Texas, and in Registration Receipts, DS, 1 July 1875 and 25 August 1875, WSM Papers.

[37]See Farrar Newberry, "Harris Flanagin," *Arkansas Historical Quarterly* 17 (Spring 1958): 3–20.

[38]In 1940, when she herself was eighty-three, Anna recalled her vivid impression of Aunt Phoebe's mule ride. See A. L. Stoner, "Explanation," AMsS, 29 April 1940, WSM Papers.

[39]*Victoria Advocate*, 28 July and 20 October 1877.

[40]Ella Hazel Atterbury Spraker, *The Boone Family: A Genealogical History of the Descendants of George and Mary Boone Who Came to America in 1717* (Rutland, VT: Tuttle Co., 1922), 286–89, 293. Information on Michael Lowery Stoner appears in Kathryn Stoner O'Connor, "George Overton Stoner, 1847–1920," TMsS, WSM Papers; Grimes, *Victoria County*, 198–201; Huson, *Refugio*, 1: 579; 2: 151–56, 167; and Rose, *Victoria*, 188–91. See also Michael L. Stoner's letters written from prison in New Orleans to his wife, Anne Elizabeth Hunt Kay Stoner, in the Simons-Stoner-Rose Papers, The Texas Collection, Baylor University, Waco, Texas.

[41]Spraker, *Boone Family*, 287–89. The wilderness exploits of "Old Mike" Stoner in Kentucky and Tennessee in the late 1700s and early 1800s are well documented. See, for instance, Spraker, *Boone Family*, 550–52; and William Henry Perrin, *History of Bourbon, Scott, Harrison and Nicholas Counties, Kentucky* (Chicago: O. L. Baskin, 1882; republished by Silas Emmett Lucas, Jr., Easley, SC: Southern Historical Press, 1979), 36–37, 84–85, 444.

[42]Letters addressed to Anaqua from Nancy Hathaway Stoner to William Clinton Stoner, 15 April and 10 June 1877, WSM Papers, indicate that Clinton Stoner was with the Cromwells in the spring of 1877. Rose, *Victoria*, 203, claims that Clinton Stoner came to Texas in 1875.

[43]Marriage license, ADS, 28 November 1877, WSM Papers.

Notes to Chapter 2

[1]Accounts of the effects of O'Connor's fence are included in Margaret Rose Warburton, "A History of the O'Connor Ranch, 1834–1839" (M.A. thesis, Catholic University of America, 1939), 67–69; and in Huson, *Refugio*, 2: 228–31. Stoner receives credit for enclosing the first pasture in Victoria County in Rose, *Victoria*, 189–91; and in Grimes, *Victoria County*, 386. McFaddin's barbed wire fence is discussed in Kathleen E. and Clifton R. St. Clair, *Little Towns of Texas* (Jacksonville, TX: Jayroe Graphic Arts, 1982), 558. Additional information on ranchers with whom the Wellingtons and Stoners had contact is recorded in Leopold Morris, "Pioneer Cattlemen of Victoria County, Texas," *The Cattleman* 34 (October 1947): 21–24.

[2]Although unnamed in the Stoner correspondence, the beekeeping journal was possibly the *American Bee Journal*, which began publication in 1861 and continues to the present. *The Household: A Monthly Journal Devoted to the Interests of the American Housewife*, published in Vermont by George E. Crowell, from 1868–1887, included articles on home management, child care, etiquette, health, and gardening, in addition to selections from literature, history, philosophy, and music. The editors also published letters from women readers covering a variety of topics. For sample excerpts from *The Household*, see Norman Justin, *So Sweet to Labor: Rural Women in America, 1865–1895* (New York: Viking Press, 1979).

[3]Refugio County, Texas, Probate Records, R. W. Wellington; Refugio County, Texas, Probate Minutes, D: 289, Refugio, Texas.

[4]Brief histories of the Lamar families mentioned in Martha's letters are included in Huson, "Two Sea Captains Johnson."

[5]Anna and Thomas related separate versions of the Victoria trip and Clinton's illness in letters to their mother. See A. L. Stoner to M. E. Wellington, 10 September 1878, and T. R. A. Wellington to M. E. Wellington, 22 August 1878, WSM Papers.

[6]The sale of the Stoners' land is recorded in Refugio County, Texas, Deeds, M: 318–20. T. R. A. Wellington sold his land to Margaret Simpson for $650. Refugio County, Texas, Deeds, M: 320. The brand is

recorded in Victoria County, Texas, Mark and Brand Book 1. Anna's brand, along with sixty-two other brands of South Texas ranchers, was included in a quilt created by her daughter-in-law, Mamie Victoria Stoner. See "Quilt Records Brands of Early Day Cattlemen," *The Cattleman* 40 (May 1953): 78.

[7]The 1880 census placed Anna and Clinton between the households of Volney J. Rose and Levin Fromme. See National Archives, Bureau of the Census, *Tenth Census, 1880, Texas*, Microcopy T-9, Roll 1330, 32: 182. See also Rose, *Victoria*, 69–70, for an 1883 record of land owners along the eastern side of the Guadalupe, most of whom are mentioned in Anna's letters.

[8]Correspondence and papers of the Volney J. Rose and Michael Lowery Stoner families are available in the Simons-Stoner-Rose Papers, The Texas Collection, Baylor University, Waco, Texas.

[9]Clinton Stoner's complex family network is delineated in Spraker, *Boone Family*, 286, 293, 393, 403.

[10]M. E. Wellington sold her 502 acres for $1,600 cash. Refugio County, Texas, Deeds, M: 479.

[11]Anna's mention of the railroad is further evidence that she lived on the east side of the Guadalupe River. In the 1880s the Gulf, Western Texas, and Pacific Railroad Company operated a train between Victoria and Port Lavaca on rails running a few miles east of and parallel to the Guadalupe. See Grimes, *Victoria County*, 521–22, and Editorial Staff, *Handbook*, 46.

[12]Although the exact phrase *a little house well-filled* does not appear in indexes of Robert Burns's works, Anna probably referred to that Scottish romantic poet, whose works were popular among nineteenth-century school girls. One of the few books Anna preserved from her school days was a volume of Burns's poetry, now part of the WSM Papers.

[13]The Stoners' granddaughter recalled that Anna's laundry routine remained unchanged into the 1920s. See McLean, *Oral Memoirs*.

[14]A. L. Stoner to M. E. Wellington, [n.d.] January, 14 February, 20 March, 27 March, 12 April, 13 May, and 4 June 1880, WSM Papers.

[15]Anna's letters record visits with relatives Maria Stoner Lynn,

Nannie H. Stoner Crawford, Zilpa Rose Stoner, Lillie Stoner Hunt, Nancy Stoner Cromwell, Lillie Blanche Rose Cromwell, Nannie Cromwell Holiday, Lee Cromwell, Mollie Gartrell, and Anne Elizabeth Hunt Kay Stoner. Likewise, she exchanged visits with Ida and Emma Hunt, Dora Fromme, Nannie Jordan, Dolly Venable, Lizzie Cunningham, and Mollie Carrothers.

[16]McLean, *Oral Memoirs*.

[17]Anna's letters provide no indication that she bought the clock she wanted in 1881. A year later, she asked her mother to purchase an inexpensive striking clock as she passed through San Antonio on her way to visit the Stoners after they moved to Edwards County. See A. L. Stoner to M. E. Wellington, 1 April 1882, WSM Papers. At the time of her death, Anna owned a Seth Thomas clock, which is now in the possession of her grandson, Royal Clinton Stoner, at the Stoner Ranch, Montell, Texas.

Notes to Chapter 3

[1]A. W. Spaight, *The Resources, Soil, and Climate of Texas* (Galveston, TX: A. H. Belo, 1882), [318].

[2]Stephen J. Arnold introduced Angoras into the Nueces River canyon in 1878; by 1883, word of Arnold's success had spread, and William Landrum moved his entire thoroughbred Angora herd into the canyon from California. A century later, in 1985, the United States was the world's second largest producer of mohair, and 97 percent of American mohair came from Texas's Edwards Plateau. Douglas E. Barnett, "Angora Goats in Texas: Agricultural Innovation on the Edwards Plateau, 1858–1900," *Southwestern Historical Quarterly* 90 (April 1987): 347, 357–58.

[3]William H. Goetzmann, *Army Exploration in the American West 1803–1863* (New Haven, CT: Yale University Press, 1959), 233–34. Huson, *Refugio*, 2: 135, 215.

[4]Deed L. Vest, "The Chihuahua Road," *Texana* 5 (Spring 1967): 4–5. Wayne R. Austerman, *Sharps Rifles and Spanish Mules: The San*

Antonio-El Paso Mail, 1851–1881 (College Station: Texas A&M University Press, 1985), 43.

[5]Vest, "Chihuahua Road," 6. Piper and his brother-in-law, George Horner, established a mercantile business in the frontier village of Uvalde in 1877. In later years, Piper and Horner's store received hides and mohair from Anna Stoner in payment for goods she bought on credit.

[6]The state of Texas, following precedent set in the days of the Republic, set aside millions of acres from the public domain for the support of state educational and charitable institutions. Proceeds from sales of state school lands endowed public schools, the University of Texas system, state orphanages, and schools for the blind, deaf, and mentally ill or handicapped.

[7]U.S. Department of the Interior, Census Office, *Statistics of the Population of the United States at the Tenth Census, June 1, 1880* (Washington, DC: Government Printing Office, 1883), 81. Spaight, *Resources, Soil, and Climate*, [317].

[8]J. Burke, Jr., comp., *Burke's Texas Almanac and Immigrant's Hand Book for 1879* (Houston, TX: J. Burke, Jr., n.d.), 91–92; and Spaight, *Resources, Soil, and Climate*, [318].

[9]Critics of personal narratives disagree concerning women's expressions of sense of place. Elizabeth A. Meese claimed that among Southern women writers "physical place offers women a unique imaginative freedom, in contrast with their otherwise restrictive circumstances," so that place becomes "a powerful metaphor for the self." Elizabeth A. Meese, "Telling It All: Literary Standards and Narratives by Southern Women," *Frontiers* 2 (Summer 1977): 65. On the other hand, Elizabeth Hampsten's research of Midwestern women's writings led her to conclude that rural women described their surroundings only to the extent that they felt estranged from them, claiming that "virtually no woman has written descriptively and remained where she was." Elizabeth Hampsten, *Read This Only to Yourself: The Private Writings of Midwestern Women, 1880–1910* (Bloomington: Indiana University Press, 1982), 226.

[10]Two more Jones children, Marie and Irene, were born after the family moved to Uvalde County. The Stoner and Jones families continued friendly relationships for three generations. For a brief history of the Jones family, see El Progreso Club, *A Proud Heritage: A History of Uvalde County, Texas* (Uvalde, TX: El Progreso Club, 1975), 374; and McLean, *Oral Memoirs*.

[11]Spraker, *Boone Family*, 394. See also Mary Margaret Stoner McLean, "Who Was Maria Stoner Lynn?," Tape recording, 2 May 1987, WSM Papers.

[12]James L. Rock and W. I. Smith, *Southern and Western Texas Guide for 1878* (St. Louis, MO: A. H. Granger, 1878), 72. See also Irene Hohmann Friedrichs, *History of Goliad* (Victoria, TX: Regal Printers, 1967).

[13]Hedwig Krell Didear, *A History of Karnes County and Old Helena* (Austin, TX: San Felipe Press, Jenkins Publishing Co., 1969), 12–17.

[14]Edward J. Dworaczyk, *The Millennium History of Panna Maria, Texas, the Oldest Polish Settlement in America 1854–1966* (n.p.: Privately printed, 1966), 78.

[15]William Foster Fleming, "San Antonio: The History of a Military City 1865–1880," (Ph.D. diss., University of Pennsylvania, 1963), 397–98.

[16]Charles Ramsdell, *San Antonio: A Historical and Pictorial Guide* (Austin: The University of Texas Press, 1959), 48–49.

[17]Over forty years later, Thomas Royal Stoner's chair hung on a nail in the house on the Stoner Ranch, and he told his children the story of his ride into the canyon in the wagon on his chair. McLean, *Oral Memoirs*.

[18]Ruth Curry Lawler, *The Story of Castroville: Its People, Founder and Traditions*, HemisFair edition (Hondo, TX: The Hondo Anvil Herald, 1968), 44.

[19]Not all women making overland journeys into the frontier went as willingly and comfortably as did Anna Wellington Stoner, but her experience was not unique. Sandra L. Myres's study of similar journeys

made in the late nineteenth century led her to conclude that the most significant outcome for families migrating overland to the West was the acquisition of new skills gained by coping with the demands of daily living on the trail, skills which proved indispensable upon reaching undeveloped destinations. See Sandra L. Myres, *Westering Women and the Frontier Experience, 1800–1915* (Albuquerque: University of New Mexico Press, 1982), 139.

[20]Information on John R. Baylor is from Allan A. Stovall, *Breaks of the Balcones: A Regional History* (Barksdale, TX: Allan A. Stovall, 1967), 122–24. Further information on the Baylor family is available in El Progreso Club, *A Proud Heritage*.

[21]Population of Montell determined from *Tenth Census, 1880, Texas*, Microcopy T-9, Roll 1330, 31: 540–41.

[22]Thomas Clubb, who settled on Montell Creek in 1875, was a former ship's pilot and lighthouse keeper on Mustang Island near Corpus Christi. See Stovall, *Breaks of the Balcones*, 122; and El Progreso Club, *A Proud Heritage*, 329–30.

Notes to Chapter 4

[1]*Texas Almanac for 1867* (Galveston, TX: W. Richardson and Co., 1866), 104.

[2]Edwards County boundaries have changed several times and now encompass twice as much area as in 1883, but still no rail line has ever crossed the county. For accounts of Indian raids and massacres in Edwards County, see Stovall, *Nueces Headwater Country: A Regional History* (San Antonio, TX: The Naylor Company, 1959), 13–41. Population data is taken from U. S. Department of the Interior, *Statistics at the Tenth Census*, 81, and National Archives, Bureau of the Census, *Tenth Census, 1880, Texas*, Microcopy T-9, Reel 1301, 10: 333–42. Despite the low number of qualified voters in the county seat election, competition between the settlements of Bull Head, Barksdale, and Leakey was so strong that citizens cast over two thousand ballots. An

eyewitness recollection of fraudulent voting at Bull Head in 1883 is included in Rocksprings Woman's Club, *Edwards County History— 1983* (San Angelo, TX: Anchor Publishing Co., 1984), 12–13.

[3]The origin of the settlement's name has been attributed both to the discovery of an old buffalo skull on top of a nearby hill and to the resemblance of the mountain that overshadows the village to the shape of a bull's head. The name later became Vance. See Allan A. Stovall's histories, *Nueces Headwater Country*, 39, and *Breaks of the Balcones*, 324.

[4]Anna's descriptions of the Stoner home in Edwards County are the only extant evidence of its location. Stovall, *Nueces Headwater Country*, 73–74, 368, provides a hint of the site's location: "In 1884, John Newman . . . bought the place at the mouth of George Perkins Hollow from a Mrs. Stoner. He sold this place later to Abe Holmes." George Perkins's land was a few miles below Hackberry. The site became part of Real County in 1913.

[5]The Stoner and Billings families remained friends for several generations. Stoner family tradition claims that Clinton Stoner served as deputy under one of the Billings brothers, who was sheriff. See: Michael Lowery Stoner, *Oral Memoirs of Michael Lowery Stoner;* and Royal Clinton Stoner, *Oral Memoirs of Royal Clinton Stoner;* typed transcripts of a series of tape-recorded interviews conducted by Lois E. Myers, in progress, Baylor University Institute for Oral History, Waco, Texas.

[6]Anna's grandsons recalled milking similar cows in the 1920s and 1930s, with little reward for a great amount of effort. See M. L. Stoner, *Oral Memoirs*, and R. C. Stoner, *Oral Memoirs*.

[7]Martha Wellington purchased Lot 10, Range 2, District 4, Bexar County, from Julia Leffering. Warranty Deed, DS, 26 September 1882, WSM Papers.

[8]Herff's accomplishments in medicine during his fifty-year practice in San Antonio were widely known. See, for instance, Frederick Charles Chabot, *With the Makers of San Antonio* (San Antonio, TX: Privately printed, 1937), 386–87, 411.

[9]The Wellingtons never recovered the items left in Victoria County. A severe wind storm in August 1886 destroyed the place where their belongings were stored and scattered them over the prairie. See Amanda Jane Williams to A. L. Stoner, 25 February 1887, WSM Papers. Fifty years later, Martha Wellington's great-granddaughter recovered some of Royal Wellington's medical books from descendants of Amanda Williams who had found them in pastures. See McLean, *Oral Memoirs*.

[10]Contrary to Anna's prediction, Edwin M. Phelps was elected to Texas's Eighteenth Legislature, representing the Eighty-seventh District (Victoria, DeWitt, Jackson, Calhoun, Refugio, Goliad, and Aransas counties). For more on Phelps's political career, see Lewis E. Daniell, *Personnel of the Texas State Government with Sketches of Representative Men of Texas* (San Antonio, TX: Maverick Printing House, 1892), 612–13.

[11]See also A. Sydney Venable to W. C. Stoner, 15 October 1882, WSM Papers.

[12]Anna's remarks are the only extant record of the loan made between Clinton and his brother Bob.

[13]The Galbraith family left the Bull Head area a year later and settled in Uvalde County near Montell, where Richard Galbraith founded the Church of the Ascension. Galbraith's younger sons founded the Foxworth-Galbraith Lumber Company, which still operates throughout Texas. See El Progreso Club, *Proud Heritage*, 351; and McLean, *Oral Memoirs*.

Notes to Afterword

[1]Stories of Anna's experiences with horse thieves in Edwards County have become part of the Stoner family oral tradition, as recounted by her grandsons in M. L. Stoner, *Oral Memoirs*, and R. C. Stoner, *Oral Memoirs*. Stovall claims that John Newman bought Anna's land in the upper canyon in *Nueces Headwater Country*, 73–74.

Anna signed the deed for her land in the lower canyon on 6 October 1884, purchasing Survey No. 174 on the east bank of the Nueces River from Robert Parsons for $800 cash and a note for $200 payable 1 April 1885. Uvalde County, Texas, Deed Records, N: 168–69, Uvalde, Texas. The post office at Good Luck was later renamed Laguna.

[2]Receipts, DS, 11 February and 20 October 1886, WSM Papers; Receipt, ADS, 1 March 1886, WSM Papers.

[3]In 1917, at the age of fifty years, Thomas Chilton Stoner, Jr., married twenty-two-year-old Mattie Lynn Crawford, the daughter of his cousin Michael Crawford, whose wife was the former Leila Jones, one of the children of William and Mattie Lynn Jones who migrated West with Clinton and Anna Stoner. Tom Stoner and his wife bought land across the Montell highway from Anna's ranch. Spraker, *Boone Family*, 398, 451; and McLean, *Oral Memoirs*.

[4]Hope Augusta Stoner Beaumont settled in Fresno and reared three daughters, Maidie, Anna Louise, and Hope. Later, she and Beaumont divorced. Hope Stoner Beaumont died on 13 June 1942, preceding her mother in death by eleven years. Spraker, *Boone Family*, 457; Ligon, *Ligon Family*, 719; and McLean, *Oral Memoirs*.

[5]Certificate of Membership, DS, 7 January 1902, WSM Papers.

[6]Spraker, *Boone Family*, 457; Ligon, *Ligon Family*, 719. For more information on Anna's descendants, see Margaret Stoner McLean, "Anna Louisa Wellington Stoner," TMs, WSM Papers; McLean, *Oral Memoirs*; M. L. Stoner, *Oral Memoirs*; and R. C. Stoner, *Oral Memoirs*.

[7]Articles have appeared through the years in local newspapers regarding Anna as a pioneer and ranch founder. See Malcolm D. McLean, "Nueces Canyon Pioneer's Early Day Experiences Described by University of Texas Professor," *Uvalde Leader-News*, 15 March 1951, p. 2A; and "Stoner Ranch Honored," *Uvalde Leader-News*, 25 November 1984, pp. 4B, 14B.

[8]O. D. Coleman to A. L. Stoner, 17 January 1937, WSM Papers.

[9]Uvalde County, Texas, Probate Proceedings, Uvalde, Texas. Thomas Royal Stoner died 28 March 1960; his wife Mamie died 22 January 1974. Both are buried near Anna in the Montell Cemetery.

Notes to Appendix

[1]Further details available in Ligon, *Ligon Family;* and Bradshaw, *Prince Edward County.*

[2]For more information, see Spraker, *Boone Family.*

Works Cited

Primary Sources

Manuscript Collections

Simons-Stoner-Rose Papers. The Texas Collection. Baylor University. Waco, Texas.

Wellington-Stoner-McLean Papers. The Texas Collection. Baylor University. Waco, Texas.

Government Documents: Federal

National Archives. Bureau of the Census. *Tenth Census, 1880, Texas.* Microfilm.

National Archives and Records Administration. *Post Office Department Reports of Site Locations, 1837–1950.* Washington, DC: National Archives and Records Administration, n.d. Microfilm Publication M1126. Photocopy.

National Archives and Records Services. *Population Schedules of the Eighth Census of the United States, 1860, Texas.* Washington, DC: National Archives, 1967. Microfilm.

——— . *Population Schedules of the Eighth Census of the United States, 1860, Texas. Slave Schedules.* Washington, DC: National Archives, 1967. Microfilm.

——— . *Population Schedules of the Ninth Census of the United States, 1870, Texas.* Washington, DC: National Archives, 1965. Microfilm.

Works Cited

U.S. Department of the Interior. Census Office. *Statistics of the Population of the United States at the Tenth Census, June 1, 1880.* Washington, DC: Government Printing Office, 1883.

Government Documents: County

Refugio County. Texas. Commissioner's Court Minutes. Refugio, Texas.
————. Probate Minutes. Refugio, Texas.
————. Probate Records. Refugio, Texas.
————. Transcribed Records of Deeds. Refugio, Texas.
Uvalde County. Texas. Records of Deeds. Uvalde, Texas.
————. Probate Proceedings. Uvalde, Texas.
Victoria County. Texas. Mark and Brand Book. Victoria, Texas.

Oral History Interviews

McLean, Mary Margaret Stoner. *Oral Memoirs of Mary Margaret Stoner McLean.* Typed transcript of a series of tape-recorded interviews conducted by Lois E. Myers. In progress. Institute for Oral History. Baylor University. Waco, Texas.
Stoner, Michael Lowery. *Oral Memoirs of Michael Lowery Stoner.* Typed transcript of a series of tape-recorded interviews conducted by Lois E. Myers. In progress. Institute for Oral History. Baylor University. Waco, Texas.
Stoner, Royal Clinton. *Oral Memoirs of Royal Clinton Stoner.* Typed transcript of a series of tape-recorded interviews conducted by Lois E. Myers. In progress. Institute for Oral History. Baylor University. Waco, Texas.

Theses and Dissertations

Fleming, William Foster. "San Antonio: The History of a Military City 1865–1880." Ph.D. diss., University of Pennsylvania, 1963.
Myers, Lois Ellen Smith. "Through a Woman's Eyes: Family Life on the Texas Frontier from the Letters of Anna Wellington Stoner, 1877–1884." M.A. thesis, Baylor University, 1988.

Works Cited

Warburton, Margaret Rose. "A History of the O'Connor Ranch, 1834–1939." M.A. thesis, Catholic University of America, 1939.

Unpublished Manuscripts

Banks, A. R. "Records of the Springhill Church Session." Transcribed by John A. Manry. TMs. Southwest Arkansas Regional Archives. Washington, Arkansas.

Huson, Hobart. "Two Sea Captains Johnson and Some of Their Friends." 1 December 1958. TMsS. Victoria Public Library. Victoria, Texas.

Secondary Sources

Books

Armitage, Susan, and Elizabeth Jameson, eds. *The Women's West.* Norman: University of Oklahoma Press, 1987.

Austerman, Wayne R. *Sharps Rifles and Spanish Mules: The San Antonio–El Paso Mail, 1851–1881.* College Station: Texas A&M University Press, 1985.

Bowden, J. J. *The Exodus of Federal Forces from Texas 1861.* Austin, TX: Eakin Press, 1986.

Bradshaw, Herbert Clarence. *History of Prince Edward County, Virginia.* Richmond, VA: Dietz Press, 1955.

Brown, Marion T. *Letters from Fort Sill 1886–1887.* Edited by C. Richard King. Austin, TX: The Encino Press, 1970.

Burke, J., Jr., comp. *Burke's Texas Almanac and Immigrant's Hand Book for 1879.* Houston, TX: J. Burke, Jr., [1879].

Chabot, Frederick Charles. *With the Makers of San Antonio.* San Antonio, TX: Privately printed, 1937.

Cott, Nancy F. *Root of Bitterness: Documents of the Social History of American Women.* New York: E. P. Dutton, 1972.

Daniell, Lewis E. *Personnel of the Texas State Government with Sketches of Representative Men of Texas.* San Antonio, TX: Maverick Printing House, 1892.

Works Cited

Didear, Hedwig Krell. *A History of Karnes County and Old Helena.* Austin, TX: San Felipe Press, Jenkins Publishing Co., 1969.

Dworaczyk, Edward J. *The Millennium History of Panna Maria, Texas, the Oldest Polish Settlement in America 1854–1966.* N.p.: Privately printed, 1966.

Editorial Staff of The Handbook of Texas, eds. *The Handbook of Victoria County.* Austin: Texas State Historical Association, 1990.

El Progreso Club. *A Proud Heritage: A History of Uvalde County, Texas.* Uvalde, TX: El Progreso Club, 1975.

Faragher, John Mack. *Women and Men on the Overland Trail.* New Haven, CT: Yale University Press, 1979.

Featherstonhaugh, G[eorge] W[illiam]. *Excursion through the Slave States, from Washington on the Potomac to the Frontier of Mexico; with Sketches of Popular Manners and Geological Notices.* New York: Harper & Brothers, 1844; reprint, New York: Negro Universities Press, 1968.

Fischer, Christiane, ed. *Let Them Speak for Themselves: Women in the American West, 1849–1900.* Hamden, CT: Archor Books, Shoe String Press, 1977.

Friedrichs, Irene Hohmann. *History of Goliad.* Victoria, TX: Regal Printers, 1967.

Goetzmann, William H. *Army Exploration in the American West 1803–1863.* New Haven, CT: Yale University Press, 1959.

Grimes, Roy, ed. *300 Years in Victoria County.* Victoria, TX: Victoria Advocate, 1968.

Hampsten, Elizabeth. *Read This Only to Yourself: The Private Writings of Midwestern Women, 1880–1910.* Bloomington: Indiana University Press, 1982.

Hart, Katherine, and Elizabeth Kemp, eds. *Lucadia Pease and the Governor: Letters, 1850–1857.* Austin, TX: The Encino Press, 1974.

Hatcher, Mattie Austin. *Letters of an Early American Traveler: Mary Austin Holley. Her Life and Her Works, 1784–1846.* Dallas: Southwest Press, 1933.

Holman, David, comp. *Letters of Hard Times in Texas 1840–1890.* Austin, TX: Roger Beacham, 1974.

Works Cited

Huson, Hobart. *Refugio: A Comprehensive History of Refugio County from Aboriginal Times to 1953.* 2 vols. Woodsboro, TX: Rooke Foundation, 1953.

Jeffrey, Julie Roy. *Frontier Women: The Trans-Mississippi West 1840–1880.* New York: Hill & Wang, 1979.

Jensen, Joan M. *With These Hands: Women Working on the Land.* Old Westbury, NY: Feminist Press, 1981.

Joseph, Mary Patrick, Sister. *Letters from the Ursuline 1852–1853: From Our Beloved Sisters who Quitted St. Mary's, April 17th, 1852, to Commence the Mission at San Antonio.* Edited by Catherine McDowell. San Antonio, TX: Trinity University Press, 1977.

Justin, Norman. *So Sweet to Labor: Rural Women in America, 1865–1895.* New York: Viking Press, 1979.

Kelley, Mary, ed. *Woman's Being, Woman's Place: Female Identity and Vocation in American History.* Boston: G. K. Hall, 1979.

Lawler, Ruth Curry. *The Story of Castroville: Its People, Founder and Traditions.* HemisFair ed. Hondo, TX: Hondo Anvil Herald, 1968.

Ligon, William D., Jr. *The Ligon Family and Connections.* Hartford, CT: Bond Press, 1947.

Luchetti, Cathy Lee. *Women of the West.* St. George, UT: Antelope Island Press, 1982.

McLane, Bobbie Jones, and Capitola Hensley Glazner, comps. *Hempstead County, Arkansas, Marriage Records, 1817–1875.* Hot Springs, AR: Privately printed, 1969.

Malsch, Brownson. *Indianola: The Mother of Western Texas.* Rev. ed. Austin, TX: State House Press, 1988.

Morris, Leopold. *Pictorial History of Victoria and Victoria County.* San Antonio, TX: Clemens Publishing Co., 1953.

Myres, Sandra L. *Westering Women and the Frontier Experience 1800–1915.* Albuquerque: University of New Mexico Press, 1982.

Niederman, Sharon. *A Quilt of Words: Women's Diaries, Letters and Original Accounts of Life in the Southwest, 1860–1960.* Boulder, CO: Johnson Books, 1988.

Perrin, William Henry. *History of Bourbon, Scott, Harrison and Nicholas Counties, Kentucky.* Chicago: O. L. Baskin, 1882; republished by Silas Emmett Lucas, Jr., Easley, SC: Southern Historical Press, 1979.

Ragsdale, Crystal Sasse. *The Golden Free Land: The Reminiscences and Letters of Women on an American Frontier.* Austin, TX: Landmark Press, 1976.

Ramsdell, Charles. *San Antonio: A Historical and Pictorial Guide.* Austin: University of Texas Press, 1959.

Refugio County History Book Committee of the Texas Extension Homemakers Council of Refugio County. *The History of Refugio County.* Dallas: Curtis Media Corp., 1985.

Riley, Glenda. *The Female Frontier: A Comparative View of Women on the Prairie and the Plains.* Lawrence: University of Kansas Press, 1988.

——. *Frontierswomen: The Iowa Experience.* Ames: Iowa State University Press, 1981.

Rock, James L., and W. I. Smith. *Southern and Western Texas Guide for 1878.* St. Louis, MO: A. H. Granger, 1878.

Rocksprings Woman's Club. *Edwards County History—1983.* San Angelo, TX: Anchor Publishing Co., 1984.

Rose, Victor M[arion]. *Some Historical Facts in Regard to the Settlement of Victoria, Texas: Its Progress and Present Status.* Laredo, TX: Daily Times Plant, 1883; republished, edited by J. W. Petty, Jr., Victoria, TX: Book Mart, 1961.

St. Clair, Kathleen E., and Clifton R. St. Clair. *Little Towns of Texas.* Jacksonville, TX: Jayroe Graphic Arts, 1982.

Schlissel, Lillian. *Women's Diaries of the Westward Movement.* New York: Schocken Books, 1982.

——, Byrd Gibbens, and Elizabeth Hampsten. *Far From Home: Families of the Westward Journey.* New York: Schocken Books, 1989.

Spaight, A. W. *The Resources, Soil, and Climate of Texas.* Galveston, TX: A. H. Belo, 1882.

Spraker, Ella Hazel Atterbury. *The Boone Family: A Genealogical History of the Descendants of George and Mary Boone Who Came to America in 1717.* Rutland, VT: Tuttle Co., 1922.

Works Cited

Stovall, Allan A. *Breaks of the Balcones: A Regional History.* Barksdale, TX: Allan A. Stovall, 1967.

————. *Nueces Headwater Country: A Regional History.* San Antonio, TX: Naylor Company, 1959.

Stratton, Joanna L. *Pioneer Women: Voices from the Kansas Frontier.* New York: Simon & Schuster, 1981.

Texas Almanac for 1867. Galveston, TX: W. Richardson and Co., 1866.

Waerenskjold, Elise. *The Lady with the Pen: Elise Waerenskjold in Texas.* Northfield, MN: Norwegian-American Historical Association, 1961; reprint, edited by C. A. Clausen, Clifton, TX: Bosque Memorial Museum, 1976.

Wakelyn, Jon L. *Biographical Dictionary of the Confederacy.* Westport, CT: Greenwood Press, 1977.

Welter, Barbara. "The Cult of True Womanhood: 1820–1860." In *The American Family in Social-Historical Perspective*, 2d ed., ed. by Michael Gordon, 313–33. New York: St. Martin's Press, 1978.

Woods, Gary Doyle, comp. *The Hicks-Adams-Bass-Floyd-Patillo and Collateral Lines, Together with Family Letters 1840–1868.* Salado, TX: Privately printed, Anson Jones Press, 1963.

Articles

Barnett, Douglas E. "Angora Goats in Texas: Agricultural Innovation of the Edwards Plateau, 1858–1900." *Southwestern Historical Quarterly* 90 (April 1987): 347–72.

Jensen, Joan M., and Darlis A. Miller. "The Gentle Tamers Revisited: New Approaches to the History of Women in the American West." *Pacific Historical Review* 49 (May 1980): 173–213.

McLean, Margaret Stoner. "Tournaments: An Account of This Early Sport in Victoria, Texas, and Neighboring Communities." *The Cattleman* 35 (September 1948): 48–49, 188–92.

Meese, Elizabeth A. "Telling It All: Literary Standards and Narratives by Southern Women." *Frontiers* 2 (Summer 1977): 63–67.

Moffatt, Walter. "Arkansas Schools, 1819–1840." *Arkansas Historical Quarterly* 12 (Summer 1953): 91–105.

Morris, Leopold. "Pioneer Cattlemen of Victoria County, Texas." *The Cattleman* 34 (October 1947): 21–24.

Newberry, Farrar. "Harris Flanagin." *Arkansas Historical Quarterly* 17 (Spring 1958): 3–20.

"Quilt Records Brands of Early Day Cattlemen." *The Cattleman* 40 (May 1953): 78.

Ramsdell, Charles W. "Presidential Reconstruction in Texas. Part III: The Restoration of State Government." *The Quarterly of the Texas State Historical Association* 12 (January 1909): 204–30.

Scott, Ann Firor. "What, Then, is the American: This New Woman?" *Journal of American History* 65 (December 1978): 3–20.

Scully, Francis J. "Across Arkansas in 1844." *Arkansas Historical Quarterly* 13 (Spring 1954): 31–51.

Stoeltje, Beverly J. " 'A Helpmate for Man Indeed': The Image of the Frontier Woman." *Journal of American Folklore* 88 (January–March 1975): 25–41.

Stokes, Allen. "Education in Young Arkansas: Spring Hill Female Academy." *Arkansas Historical Quarterly* 27 (Summer 1968): 103–14.

Stowe, Steven M. "Growing Up Female in the Planter Class." *Helicon Nine: The Journal of Women's Arts and Letters* (Spring 1987): 195–205.

Vest, Deed L. "The Chihuahua Road." *Texana* 5 (Spring 1967): 1–10.

Index